Mandir

Faith | Form | Func...

Mandir
Faith | Form | Function

By

Sadhu Amrutvijaydas

Swaminarayan Aksharpith
Ahmedabad

Mandir
Faith | Form | Function

Inspirer: HDH Pramukh Swami Maharaj

1st Edition: August 2014

Copies: 5,000

Price: ₹ 150/-
(Reduced from ₹ 180/- by courtesy of Swaminarayan Aksharpith)

ISBN: 978-81-7526-680-3

Published & Printed by
Swaminarayan Aksharpith
Shahibaug Road, Ahmedabad-4
Gujarat, India.

Website: www.baps.org

Pramukh Swami Maharaj performs *murti-pratishtha arti*,
BAPS Shri Swaminarayan Mandir, Houston, TX, USA, 25 July 2004

Dedication

To *guruhari* His Holiness Pramukh Swami Maharaj:
Master builder of mandirs, both traditional and modern.
Guardian of the Akshar-Purushottam doctrine
revealed by Bhagwan Swaminarayan and
first enshrined by Brahmaswarup Shastriji Maharaj.
Inspirer, through these mandirs, of
Hindu traditions, values, beliefs, devotion,
and service to God and mankind.
May he forever continue to build such
marvellous edifices for the uplift of humanity.

Pramukh Swami Maharaj's
BLESSINGS

A mandir is a centre for attaining God.

A mandir is that which calms the mind.

A mandir is that which gives paramount peace.

A mandir is that which inspires a virtuous life.

A mandir is that which teaches mutual respect.

A mandir is that which protects the lofty traditional values.

A mandir is that which strengthens our original identity [as *atma*].

Bhagwan Swaminarayan incarnated on this earth and built mandirs to forever preserve the worship of Akshar-Purushottam. In them he consecrated the devas and avatars of the Sanatan Dharma and taught that all faiths should be respected. Shastriji Maharaj and Yogiji Maharaj consecrated the murtis of the eternal principles of Brahman and Parabrahman as propagated by Bhagwan Swaminarayan. They established Satsang centres in India and abroad.

With prayers to Bhagwan Swaminarayan that all continue to gain benefit from this supreme and divine work.

Blessings and Jai Swaminarayan from
Shastri Narayanswarupdas
(Pramukh Swami Maharaj)

PREFACE

Sanatan Dharma, widely known as Hinduism, is regarded by many as the world's oldest living religion. Hinduism is also regarded a way of life; it is a harmonious mosaic of doctrines and values, rituals and traditions, sciences and arts. Hindus worldwide, regardless of profession or status, incorporate these principles into their daily life.

Over the millennia, the religious traditions and beliefs of the Hindus have been preserved and spread through their mandirs, shastras and pious sadhus . These three components are regarded by many as the pillars of Hindu practice. Through natural and manmade adversities, mandirs, shastras and sadhus have been a constant source of comfort, guidance and strength. Sadhus are revered and their darshan is eagerly sought. Shastras are read and their messages discussed. Mandirs are built and *murtis* consecrated. Even today, these three pillars are the bedrocks that sustain and nourish Hinduism throughout the world.

The focus of this publication is mandirs. Although they are the most visible of the three pillars, mandirs are inextricably linked with the other two less apparent components of shastras and sadhus. This relationship is evident because mandirs are built on the basis of a body of sacred texts and infused with the presence of the divine through rituals performed by enlightened sadhus. Since antiquity, these sacred structures have continuously expressed the spiritual aspirations of the Hindu mind, visibly revealing the faith of Hindus. Despite this, the complex history, symbolism, and forms of mandirs have often remained mysterious to the casual viewer.

Thus, the purpose of this book is to demystify the meanings and forms of the Hindu mandir. By charting the meanings of symbolic visual form, as well as spiritual function, this introductory book provides a framework for understanding how mandirs have developed throughout history.

Ultimately, *Mandir: Faith, Form, Function*, traces how the *faith* of Hindus gave *form* to mandirs, at first primitive and then more sophisticated, and the *function* of these mandirs in the spiritual and social development of individuals and society.

- Author

ACKNOWLEDGEMENTS

I wish to humbly acknowledge my debt to guru Pramukh Swami Maharaj for his inspiration and blessings. My deep appreciations to Pujya Ishwarcharandas Swami and Vivekjivandas Swami for their continual encouragement and guidance in the research, writing and production of this book.

Also, my sincere gratitude to the many who have contributed and permitted the use of their photographs and illustrations in this book. Unless stated otherwise the photos are by Yogicharandas Swami, Shrijiswarupdas Swami, and BAPS youths of the audio-visual departments in India, UK and USA.

Appreciations to the following for generously permitting the use of their photographs:

- Shay Bertling (pages 33, 74)
- Jalendar Vasan (p. 28)
- ADI Tour (p. 72)
- Touristlink.com (p. 45)
- ISKCON, Ahmedabad (pages 10, 142) and Bangalore (pages 138, 140, 143, 148)
- Darshanam Sanskrit Mahavidyalaya run by Shree Swaminarayan Gurukul Vishwavidya Paristhanam (p. 13)
- To all the photographers who have uploaded their photographs to Wikipaedia and other sites under the Creative Commons Licence (pages 29, 37, 58, 79, 82, 90, 102, 122).

- Author

A NOTE ON NOMENCLATURE

Different faiths refer to their places of worship by specific words. For example, Buddhists use pagoda, Christians use church, Jains use *derasar*, Jews use synagogue, Muslims use mosque and Sikhs use *gurudwara*. Similarly, Hindus have not only one term but many to refer to their places of worship. These include: *deul, devalaya, mandir, prasada, sthanam, vihara, vimana* and many others. Of these terms, 'mandir' has become widely utilized in describing a Hindu temple. The Oxford English Dictionary defines 'mandir' as 'a building devoted to the worship, or regarded as the dwelling place, of a god or gods or other objects of religious reverence'.

Throughout this book we will use the word 'mandir' since it is one of the most popularly used by Hindus.

The terminology used to describe the architectural elements of Hindu mandirs can, at times, be confusing. This is due to the use of the same word to refer to different elements and also different words being used to describe the same element.Hence, there is much variation in terminology in the different regions of India. In this book, an attempt has been made to use the *nagara* terminology employed in the Gujarat region. However, where required, *dravida* terminology and other region-specific vocabulary has been used.

CONTENTS

1

Framework of Faith

God has always occupied a central focus in the minds of all humanity. People of all eras have had great respect, reverence and awe for the divine. In fact, as Voltaire declared, "If God did not exist, it would be necessary to invent him." For, man is not merely this visible material body. Each person is animated by a soul, an eternal spirit, which infuses each atom of the physical body with life. The end of a body's physical existence is merely another stage in the soul's quest to experience the eternal bliss of God. And, just as the soul pervades the body, God, the Supreme Spirit, pervades the soul. So, as Pierre Teilhard de Chardin, a French philosopher and Jesuit priest (1881-1955), so aptly described, "We are not human beings having a spiritual experience, but spiritual beings having a human experience." Yet, human frailties and impulses prevent man from experiencing the divinity within. Although present within, God remains tantalizingly beyond humankind's grasp.

However, over the ages, men and women of exceptional spiritual capacity have endeavoured single-mindedly throughout their lives and shown the way to God-realization. They have shown that the path of devotion is the best, most direct route to God.

Since the creation of the very first Vedic hymn till today the Indian subcontinent has passed through phases of prosperity and persecution, neglect and revival, growth and diversification. And still, Indic culture has remained absorbed in the sacred.

At first, primitive man experienced the awesome power of nature – both constructive and destructive. This led to an understanding that he was helpless before it. So, in an attempt to appease, even

Facing page:
Hindus have expressed their faith by building mandirs in a multitude of locations. Here, murtis under a tree in Suchindram, Tamil Nadu, are covered in saffron

Devotees offer worship at a local mandir

control, the forces of nature, man made symbols of the various elements of nature. Using pictures and images made of clay, grass, wood and other basic materials, man directed and focused his thoughts on them, and offered prayers.

Such devotion and contemplation led man to the realization that beyond the natural was the supernatural. So, he made images to represent his perceptions of this divine, invisible power. These images were regarded as sacred and to emphasize this, shrines of clay, wood and bamboo were built around them. These were the early mandirs, sacred spaces where people gathered to offer their prayers. Experience taught man that structures of such perishable materials had only a short life span. As a result, they were replaced with more robust structures of bricks and then stones. Gradual development led to more sophisticated and intricate designs and to the mandirs that have survived up to the present era.

Thus, the *murtis,* or embodied images of the divine, and the mandirs which house them are revered and serve to spark the latent spirituality in man. This tradition of worship has been preserved since primitive times. But, primitive does not mean backward or outdated; it refers to ancient man's natural, original and authentic expression of faith in the divine. Such faith is as relevant and

A small mandir on the
coast overlooking
the Arabian Sea, Diu

necessary even in today's postmodern era. This faith is represented in the form of mandirs of various types and these mandirs function to nurture the spiritual needs of society.

Whether an unkempt rickshaw driver or a smart company executive, a mischievous schoolboy or a hardworking housewife in India, all, at some time in the day, offer worship to their chosen deity. The worship may merely consist of a few hastily mumbled mantras outside a mandir gate or a lengthy puja with all its elaborate rites; whatever it may be, the Hindu mind in all its complexity and diversity remains focused on venerating the divine, since the sacred is held in highest esteem.

Hinduism is a broad path leading to ultimate liberation – *moksha* – from the transmigratory cycle of birth, death and re-birth. Many lanes and roads join the main route. It accepts all sorts of honest human enquiry and sadhanas for the Truth, the Sacred, the Divine.

Mandirs have played a central role in this quest. They cater for both young and old, rich and poor, intellectuals and illiterates. Through the millennia they have sustained and integrated India's diverse spirituality. Mandirs have served as a vibrant and protective heart, steadily nourishing the people with a spirituality that has survived through daunting challenges.

From serene mountain-tops
to noisy roadsides, mandirs in
various locations demonstrate
the ubiquity of mandirs in
India and mandir-centric
mindset of its people

Hindu mandirs are not merely places of worship, but are also social institutions, playing an important role in not just the religious life of the people but also in their social, cultural and economic lives. In fact, at one time, the mandir stood firm as the mother symbol of the Hindu welfare state.

The Hindus' love of mandirs has not diminished over the centuries, for mandirs enshrine their faith in the sacred. Mandirs are an external representation of their faith in God and these mandirs then sustain and enhance that faith. Indeed, everywhere in India, and now across the world, Hindu mandirs are being built and consecrated. Some remain true to ancient traditions, while others alter styles according to available resources, local building laws and weather conditions. The faithful flock to these mandirs for darshan of the sacred *murtis* consecrated within, offer prayers and receive blessings.

Today, we live in a world that pays homage to science, with modern life becoming increasingly dependent on technology. However, mandirs, *murti* worship and all the accompanying rites and rituals continue to remain relevant, probably even more so today. The divine power in mandirs continues to revitalize the thoughts and lives of countless spiritual seekers.

The saga of the evolution of the mandir represents the development of Hinduism's philosophical ideas and visions of life. It takes us on a voyage through the unfolding of Hindus' spiritual thoughts in their quest for the eternal Truth.

In addition to the grand mandirs historically patronized by royalty, there are countless smaller shrines that reflect the faith of Hindus. These small shrines are informal and not bound by textual regulations, unlike the grand formal edifices that follow a well-developed body of architectural canons. Throughout India, such informal shrines of all shapes and sizes are found in cities and villages, under trees and bridges, on the roadside and on the road, by rivers and by railway tracks, in built-up neighbourhoods and in homes – in fact, mandirs are ubiquitous and have been an integral part of the Indic landscape for many centuries. Their pervasive presence reflects the unshakeable faith that characterizes Hindus.

This co-existence of both the grand and simple, formal and informal, traditional and modern aptly reflects the open and unrestricted mandir tradition of Hinduism, which, in the form of worship towards different deities, accommodates a multitude of approaches to reaching the Divine.

2

The Mandir as Sacred Space

Religious architecture represents sacred space amid this profane world and has always played a pivotal role in the history of humankind. In fact, many of the extant ancient monuments found throughout the world today have an underlying religious dimension, since, over the course of human history, all religious faiths have initiated and improved upon the construction of their places of worship. These grand physical structures naturally draw one's attention, and so it is important to appreciate the significance, sentiments and symbolism that these sacred spaces and places represent.

Sacred spaces command tremendous power, for they are where the divine dwells. This does not mean that the gods are confined to only this place; although they are present here, they are omnipresent and so transcend the earthly sphere, simultaneously being present in their own heavenly realm.

Essentially, since they are isolated from the humdrum and chaos of everyday distractions and difficulties, sacred places stimulate meditation on the divine, encourage spiritual enquiry, preserve rituals and facilitate devotional acts for spiritual seekers endeavouring to attain spiritual enlightenment. Religion in general, and sacred spaces in particular, are relief valves that help man to release his daily pressures and pains, and preserve his all-round well-being.

Since early times, humans have innately realized that life extends beyond the visible, and have postulated a 'sacred dimension' in addition to this physical realm. However, this sacred or divine

Facing page:
Grand gates mark the interface between the peaceful spiritual world of the mandir and the commotion of the world outside

Repetitve carved designs
signify the infinity
of creation.

Carving depicting victory
of Lord Nrusinh over the
evil King Hiranyakashipu

domain is not directly accessible by the five physical senses. So, humans require assistance in order to experience the divine; this is facilitated by sacred spaces and places.

For Hindus, mandirs – edifices in honour of God – constitute such sacred space and are an undeniable statement of their faith in and devotion to God, since the sheer effort needed to build and sustain them in terms of time and resources is not possible otherwise.

Visually and spiritually, mandirs represent divine power and attract people by their beauty and grandeur. Such grand mandirs emphasize the gulf between almighty God and powerless humans, and distinguish between the sacred and the profane on earth. Mandirs serve to fulfil the spiritual needs of man and provide a medium through which one can know and understand God and evolve spiritually to attain the divine.

To gain a spiritual understanding of the world, man needs to detach from the world and retreat within to reflect. Mandirs facilitate such contemplation, and the results of such insights enable man to approach the divine, develop meaning to life and experience peace.

A mandir is a house of God and so provides an appropriate atmosphere to be in the presence of God. It is regarded as a scaled-

Sculptures of avatars,
sages and devotees
inspire devotees

down model of the cosmos where devotees can offer devotion, service and prayers and direct their reverence to God.

Further, not only is it a place of worship, but it is also an object of worship. It is where the divine is endowed with a form. The sculpture-seers of ancient India conceived mandirs not as mere buildings, but as sacred representations of God. And so each part is imbued with unique significance and meaning, unveiled only to the discerning devotee.

Mandirs are well demarcated from the material world, often by a decorated entrance gate and enclosure walls, which physically and symbolically separate the mandir from the outside world. The soaring height of the mandir draws the mind towards the infinite beyond the physical realm. The height also serves to give the mandir prominence among the surrounding structures, and symbolizes man's attempt to transcend the mundane and touch the divine. This subtle symbolism reminds the seeker that endeavour is essential to reach the divine.

Also, the repetition of various forms conveys the idea of the infinity of objects, while the images of gods, sages, devotees and others display the connection of the mandir with the physical world. The mandir provides devotees a tangible form to contemplate upon

Sculpture of Shiva dancing
in the form of Natraj

A priest performs *arti*

A devotee offers *abhishek* to a Shivalinga

and rouses the latent qualities within that will liberate one from worldly attachments and facilitate spiritual progress.

Mandirs contribute to the universal search for meaning and encourage enquiry into life's most profound questions: Who are we? Where did we come from? Why are we here? Where are we going? What do we have to do? Through their symbolism, mandirs enable communication of concepts that provide answers to these and many other questions.

By entering a mandir one enters a world of rich symbolic narratives and messages – some clear, some cryptic – that trigger an experience of the sacred and divine, and give meaning and purpose to life. While the use of traditional symbols helps to communicate these ancient concepts, the resulting art creates a welcoming atmosphere that encourages serene and unhurried contemplation, and aids significantly in one's worship and experience of the sacred.

However, for present day visitors, it is necessary to appreciate the spirit and circumstances of the era in which the mandir was built to fully understand the symbolism. The art and sculpture in some mandirs depict the way of life at the time and include scenarios of warfare, marriage, romance and entertainment.

Devotees sing devotional songs under the main dome of a mandir

The need for sacred places arose due to the popularity of religious rituals and devotional acts. Mandirs are a home to such rituals – purposeful sacred actions which help a seeker to engage with God through body, mind and soul and experience his presence. Involvement in collective spiritual activities empowers individuals and enhances their spiritual practices. They enable a community to feel the presence of transcendent God and collectively experience divinity. They help to focus the mind on spiritual matters and enable teachings to be put into practice.

Mandirs are a venue for individual and collective worship and impart whatever is good to all who come. They facilitate integration of the worship community and also educate the young regarding their traditions and values, which may be from the past, but continue to inspire in the present and lay the foundations for the future. Repeated exposure to these sacred actions and symbols gradually results in a more profound understanding and experience.

Young children engaged in darshan during a visit to a mandir

Mandirs focus one's attention onto the divine, since they are designed to facilitate devotion. From entry through the main gate up to the sanctum sanctorum, the seeker embarks on a journey from initiation to enlightenment. The various buildings which are traversed to reach the sanctum symbolize the progress of a devotee

Devotees pray inside a mandir compound

on his spiritual journey. At the main gateway, the devotee first humbly bows down and touches the threshold before crossing it. This indicates that the passage from the mundane to the godly has begun. Mandirs teach, nurture and encourage specified ways of living that will take one to the divine. Though this does not prevent people from displaying their mundaneness, sincere endeavours to correct one's wayward manners does result in improvement and helps one to overcome one's base natures and experience divinity.

Only through active involvement of the community can mandirs be established and nurtured. Hence, mandirs are not detached from the community, but play an integral role in sustaining and developing it. The greater the active engagement, the stronger the affiliation and the greater the experience of divinity.

Building such mandirs enables necessary distribution of economic resources and so helps in sustaining society. Moreover, association with and participation in the construction and sustenance of such mandirs enables man to earn God's grace and gain freedom from the shackles of mundane existence.

A mandir benefits not only those who worship in it but also the vicinity in which it is located. In day-to-day life, long daily journeys are not practical for the vast majority of people. Hence,

Resident student youths of a *gurukul* perform Vedic *homa* rituals

Darshanam

mandirs are built for the convenience and easy accessibility of devotees, resulting in many local mandirs of differing sizes and grandeur.

So, whether they pierce the sky with glittering *kalashes* or are just topped by precariously balanced thatched roofs, mandirs are living dedications to the Supreme. They are a source of peace, joy and comfort.

3

Mandir Structure Overview

The mandir is, in essence, the home of God. Initially, a mandir comprised of only a cella, a simple cube structure covered by a flat roof. This was the sanctum sanctorum. Also known as the *garbhagruha*, or womb-house, the sanctum is where the image of God is consecrated. All other constructions within the mandir compound are secondary to it. From around the 4th century CE onwards, as requirements changed, additional buildings were added to this basic cube form. Despite the vast and varied territory of the country, mandir architecture is surprisingly similar, since it follows common fundamental rules for construction. At the same time, depending on the region of the country, there is also much variation in the structure of the various parts that constitute a mandir and its supporting structures, and the terminology used to describe them.

The mandir proper, called the *garbhagruha* or sanctum, houses the divine deity. The sanctum is dark and has only one opening – the entrance door, usually on the eastern side. All other additional components of the mandir complex are built along the horizontal and vertical planes with reference to the *garbhagruha*.

HORIZONTAL DEVELOPMENT

As the number of devotees visiting mandirs and the variety of rituals performed increased, *mandaps* (halls) were built in front of the *garbhagruha*. The halls have either walls with windows or doors to let in light and air, or are open and may have railings. Usually, they contain sculpted pillars and have intricately designed ceilings.

The *mahamandap*, located in front of the *garbhagruha* and from

Facing page:
A small simple *rekha deul* (*garbhagruha*) with the basic structural components of a typical mandir, Bhuvaneshwar, Odisha

Garbhagruha   Antara

Note: The colour of the mandir in this photograph has been digitally modified to highlight the different elements of a mandir

Mahamandap

Mandap

Ardhamandap

Shikhar

Chhaju

Jangha

Mandovar

Kanpith

Bhit (Pith)

Note: The colour of the mandir in this photograph has been digitally modified to highlight the different elements of a mandir

where devotees have darshan of the consecrated *murti*, was at first a separate building, with open space between it and the *garbhagruha*. Later, the two structures became connected by an intermediate passage or vestibule called the *antarala,* also known as *korimandap*. Leading up to the *mahamandap* is an *ardhamandap* or *roop choki*, which is an open, pillared porch at the front or to the sides of the *mahamandap*. In design and carving it resembles the *mahamandap*.

Surrounding the *garbhagruha*, paths – covered or open – were added to enable circumambulation (*pradakshina*). Mandirs with a circumambulatory path are known as *sandhara*; those without such a path are called *nirandhara*.

The *garbhagruha* and *mandaps* have individual ceilings and are generally topped by *shikhars* (pinnacles) or *ghummats* (domes); the *shikhars* or domes built on top of the additional *mandaps* are smaller than the main *shikhar* on the *garbhagruha*. Sometimes subsidiary shrines, with superstructures, on raised platforms are also built to house associated deities.

In the courtyard surrounding the mandir there may be a water tank for ritual purposes. Finally, predominantly in South India, the mandir may be enclosed by a perimeter wall with a *gopuram* (decorated gate).

The ground plan on which the mandir is built – square, rectangle, circle or other – is a feature of the mandir style.

VERTICAL DEVELOPMENT

The mandir may be built on an *adhisthana* (plinth), on top of which is the *vedibandha* – the socle, or immediate base, of the mandir structure. This may be plain or have several bands of decorative mouldings featuring designs, such as, flowers, geometric shapes, horses, elephants, human figures and others. The socle links and supports the base to the *jangha* (wall) of the *garbhagruha*.

The wall is capped by a cornice (*chhaju* or *varandika*) or a series of cornice mouldings, above which rises the *shikhar* – the superstructure, spire or pinnacle. The *shikhar* is a tower-like structure whose design varies according to the mandir style. There are three main mandir styles, which will be discussed in the next chapter. The *shikhar* is crowned by a *kalash* and flagpole. Mandirs of North India generally describe the sanctum and *shikhar* separately, whereas in South India the sanctum-*shikhar* combination is referred to as a *vimana*.

4

Mandir Styles

The architectural styles which originated in the 4th to 6th centuries CE were further developed during the Indian medieval period (generally regarded as from 6th to 16th centuries CE) throughout the whole of the country.

As a result of the detailed studies of thousands of mandirs all over India, scholars have identified four salient features which determine a mandir's architectural style: (1) superstructure, (2) ground plan, (3) wall surface designs and (4) 'order' – pillar structure and sculpture. Of these, the most important distinguishing feature of a mandir is its superstructure.

There are three main Hindu mandir styles: (1) *nagara*, or North Indian style, (2) *dravida*, South Indian Style and (3) *vesara*, or the mixed style, found in Karnataka and the Deccan. Each of these styles is predominantly, but not exclusively, associated with certain geographical regions of India (see map on p. 22) and has numerous sub-styles, resulting in a rich diversity of constructions.

Commenting on this classification, mandir architecture scholar, Adam Hardy, says, "*Nagara* and *dravida* should be understood as architectural languages, in the sense that they provide a vocabulary, a range of elements, and a family of forms which can be put together in different ways." He also advocates that the term 'Karnata-Dravida' is a better title than *vesara* for the mixed-style mandirs of the Deccan.

NAGARA (NORTHERN) STYLE

Mandirs of the *nagara* style are found extensively in the area from the Himalayas in the north to the Deccan plateau and Madhya

*Facing page:
Mandirs at Pattadakal,
Karnataka: the near shrine
is of the dravida style
and the farther shrine is
of the nagara style*

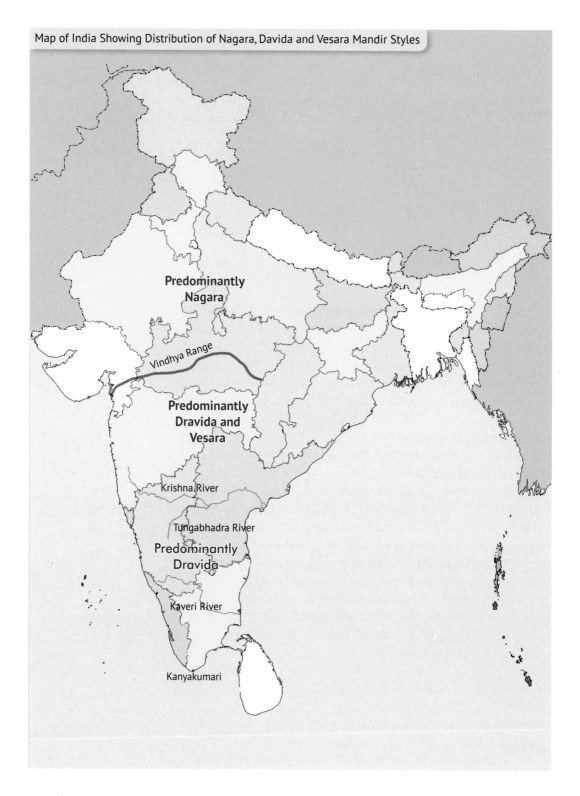

Map of India Showing Distribution of Nagara, Davida and Vesara Mandir Styles

Predominantly
Nagara

Vindhya Range

Predominantly
Dravida and
Vesara

Krishna River

Tungabhadra River

Predominantly
Dravida

Kaveri River

Kanyakumari

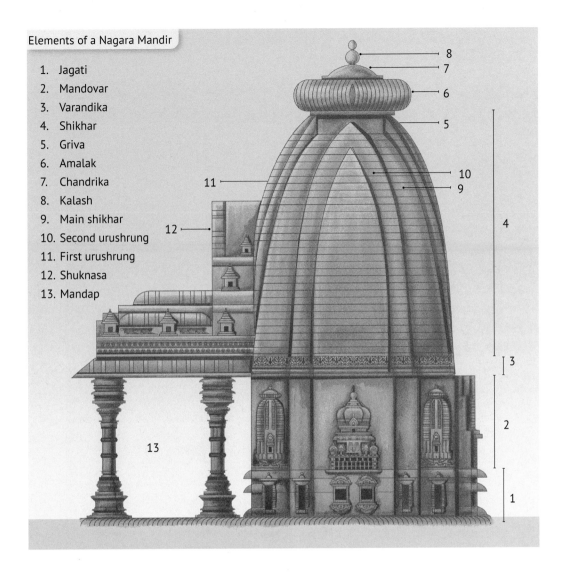

Elements of a Nagara Mandir

1. Jagati
2. Mandovar
3. Varandika
4. Shikhar
5. Griva
6. Amalak
7. Chandrika
8. Kalash
9. Main shikhar
10. Second urushrung
11. First urushrung
12. Shuknasa
13. Mandap

Pradesh in the south, and from Gujarat in the west to the shores of Orissa in the east. They are also found as far south as the Tungabhadra Valley in Karnataka.

Due to the spread of this style over such vast territories, many regional variations developed, while maintaining a basic uniformity in essential features. Influenced by powerful ruling dynasties, regional variations developed in Bihar, Bengal, central India, Gujarat, Kashmir, Orissa, Rajasthan and Uttar Pradesh.

Nagara mandirs have a characteristic curvilinear corn-cob shaped *shikhar* built on a cruciform ground plan. The *shikhar* is typically crowned by a round stone disk with ridges on the rim, called an

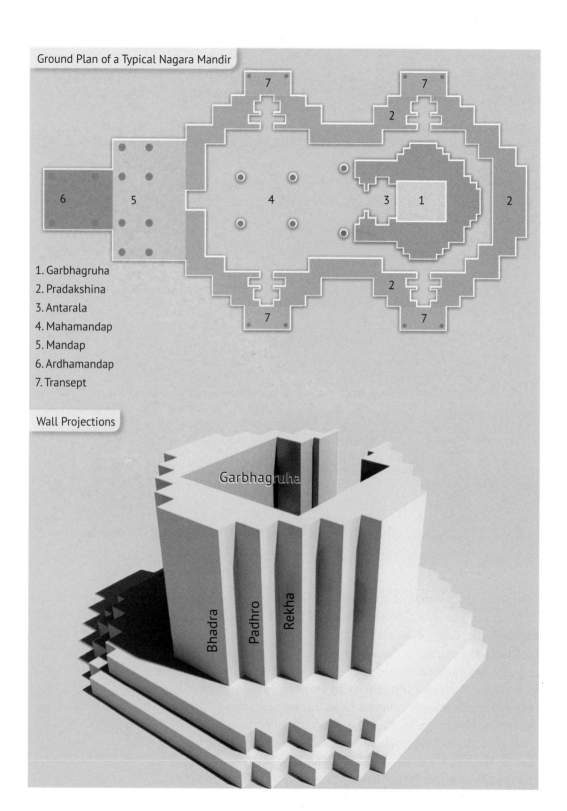

Ground Plan of a Typical Nagara Mandir

7
7
2
6 | 5 | 4 | 3 | 1 | 2
2
7 | 7
2

1. Garbhagruha
2. Pradakshina
3. Antarala
4. Mahamandap
5. Mandap
6. Ardhamandap
7. Transept

Wall Projections

Garbhagruha

Bhadra
Padhro
Rekha

amalak, and on top of this is the *kalash* (water pitcher). The *garbha-gruha* of a *nagara* mandir is often called 'prasada' or 'mula-prasada'.

The outer walls of the *garbhagruha* may feature one, three, and sometimes more projections, which extend all the way from the base of the mandir up the walls to the top of the *shikhar*. Thus, there is a clear focus on vertical lines in the mandir's elevation. The central projection, called *bhadra*, is the largest and generally features a *murti* in a niche; the other projections, called *rathas*, are often decorated with statues. A mandir with one projection on each wall, is called 'triratha' (since it results in three separate outer surfaces for embellishing the walls), two projections – 'pancharatha' (five surfaces), three projections – 'saptharatha' (seven surfaces) and four projections – 'navaratha' (nine surfaces). In the Gujarat *nagara* nomenclature, the second projection is called *padhro* and the third is called *rekha* (see bottom illustration on p. 24).

The cruciform plan and curvilinear *shikhar* became evident in *nagara* mandirs from the 6th century CE, i.e. from the late Gupta era; for example, the Dashavatar Mandir at Deogarh. The beginning of the typical *nagara shikhar* can be seen in the 7th century Mahadev Mandir at Nachna Kuthara and the mature *nagara* style is apparent by the 8th century.

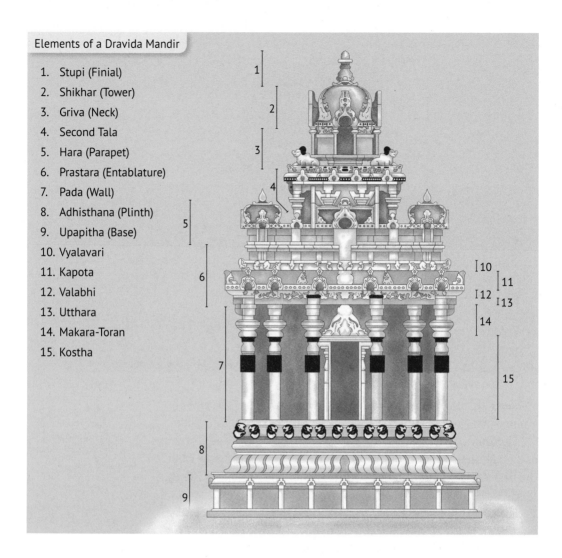

Elements of a Dravida Mandir

1. Stupi (Finial)
2. Shikhar (Tower)
3. Griva (Neck)
4. Second Tala
5. Hara (Parapet)
6. Prastara (Entablature)
7. Pada (Wall)
8. Adhisthana (Plinth)
9. Upapitha (Base)
10. Vyalavari
11. Kapota
12. Valabhi
13. Utthara
14. Makara-Toran
15. Kostha

Northern style mandirs also feature niches with sculptures, distinctive column designs, and internal domes in the *mahamandap* and *ardhamandap*.

Among the best examples of the North Indian style of mandir architecture are the Khajuraho group of mandirs, Surya Mandir in Konark and Surya Mandir in Modhera.

DRAVIDA (SOUTHERN) STYLE

The *dravida* style is most prevalent in the region between the Krishna River and Kanyakumari. *Dravidian* architecture originated around the 6th century CE in Tamil Nadu and also flourished in the southern states of Karnataka, Kerala and Andhra Pradesh. Its

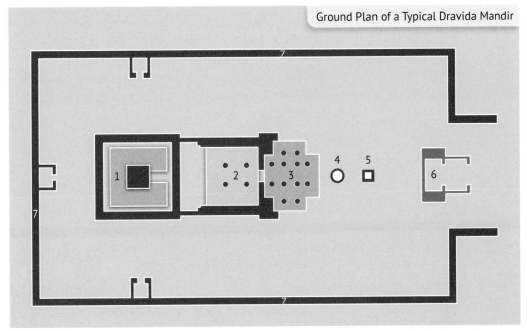

1. Garbhagruha
2. Mandap with pillars
3. Ardhamandap with multiple staircases
4. Dhvajasthambha
5. Balipith
6. Gopuram
7. Perimeter wall

development was vigourously supported by the principal royal dynasties that ruled in southern India over the centuries: Pallavas, Cholas, Pandyas, Cheras, Chalukyas, Rashtrakutas, Hoysalas, Vijayanagaras and Nayakas.

Dravida mandirs are built on a square plan and have ornate pyramidal *shikhars* assembled using mouldings arranged in tiers.

The sanctum (known as *vimana*) is surrounded by thick walls that, together with their moulded plinth and parapet, form the first tier (*tala*) of a stepped pyramid. The sanctum has a pyramidal, storied superstructure. The spire consists of an arrangement of gradually receding storeys (*bhumis*) in a pyramidal shape. The parapet around this pyramid also has miniature shrines arranged in a series: square ones (*kutas*) at the corners and rectangular ones (*salas*) in the centre. The space between them is bridged by miniature wall elements called *harantaras* (rows of miniature shrines). On top of the stepped structure is a neck (*griva*) that supports a solid dome, or cupola (instead of the *nagara* grooved disc), which in turn is crowned by a pot and finial. This emphasis on horizontal lines contrasts with the vertical focus of *nagara* mandirs.

Another distinguishing feature of the South Indian mandir style is the huge *gopurams* or mandir gateways. Based on an oblong plan, they consist of multiple storeys, culminating in a crowning

Jalendar Vasan

Dravida style: Kailasnath Mandir, Kanchipuram, Tamil Nadu

element called the 'stupi' or 'stupika'. Two storeys are separated from each other by horizontal mouldings. Like the *vimana*, it also has a pyramidal superstructure adorned with *haras*. It is crowned by a barrel vault roof along with a row of *stupis* (finials). Sometimes these gateways are taller and more decorative than the main mandir.

The *prakaras* (enclosure, or boundary, walls) are another important feature of South Indian, *dravida*, mandirs, and enclose the main shrine and other structures of the mandir complex.

Thick columns, a well or bathing tank, *bali pith, dhvajasthambha* (flagpole) and *dipasthambha* are also features of South Indian, *dravidian* style, mandirs.

Among the finest examples of the *dravidian* style are the mandirs at Thanjavur, Madurai, Mahabalipuram, Badami, Pattadakal, Kanchipuram and Hampi (Vijayanagara).

As it was prevalent over a much smaller geographical region than the *nagara* style, the *dravida* style has less variation in its architectural features and overall appearance.

VESARA

The third architectural style which emerged during the early medieval period is *vesara*, a fusion of the *nagara* and *dravida* styles.

It is found in the area between the Vindhyas and the Krishna River. The mixture of northern and southern elements resulted in many variations. This trend of combining the two styles was introduced by the Chalukyas of Badami (500-735 CE) and was further developed by the Rashtrakutas of Manyakheta (750-983 CE) in Ellora, the Chalukyas of Kalyani (983-1195 CE) in Lakkundi, Dambal, Gadag and then by the Hoysalas (1000-1330 CE). Most of the mandirs built in Halebid, Belur and Somnathpura are classified under this style.

The *vesara* style often makes use of a star-shaped ground plan and its curved pyramidal tower comprises features of both the *nagara* and *dravida* styles. It gives emphasis to elaborate carvings on the walls, decorative ceilings, lathe-turned pillars and sculptured *vimanas*.

In addition to the variation in structure, the terminology to describe the architectural components also varies according to the region. The Vishwakarma and Maya schools of mandir architecture provide the basis for the terminology of the two main styles of Hindu mandirs: the *nagara* style derives its terminology from the Vishwakarma School, while the *dravida* style derives its terminology from the Maya School.

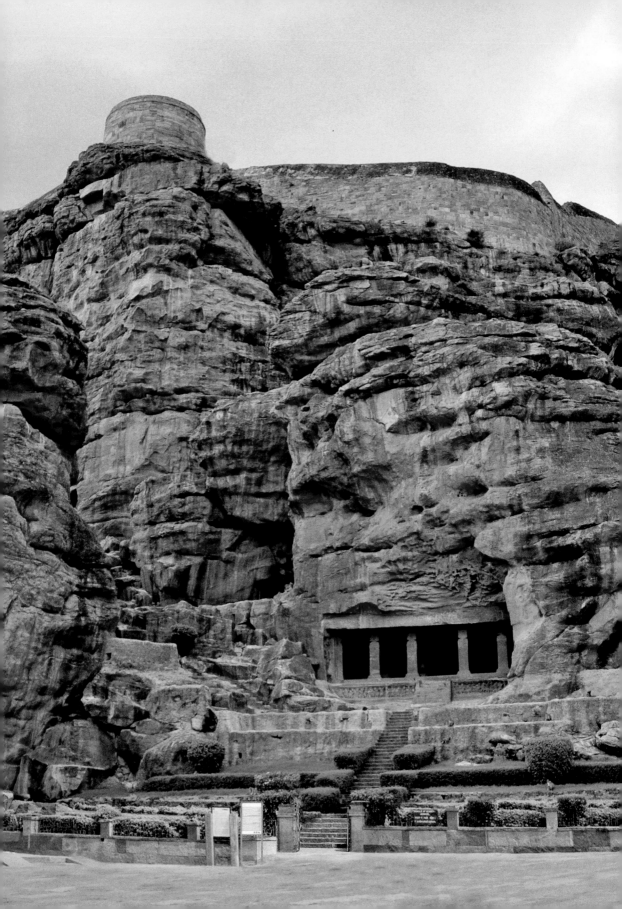

5

Early Mandirs

India is the home of mandirs. Its vast terrain is, in fact, a vibrant and ever-expanding museum of ancient and modern mandirs. Since the Vedic era, Hindus have always given prominence to rituals, devotion and places of worship.

In Vedic times, sacrificial rituals were the mainstay of devotion, for which open-air enclosures, *yagna* altars, were meticulously constructed, based on the details specified by the *Shulbasutras*. These *yagna* altars were readily erected under trees or near water bodies and other natural landmarks to perform Vedic rituals, and were dismantled afterwards. However, the natural landmark, such as a tree or rock, around which the altar was built served as a reminder of the sanctity of the site.

In addition to performing *yagnas*, the Vedic people worshipped nature in all its variety: water, sun, trees, mountains and even some animals. They viewed them as representations of the divine and gave them a physical form. These were the early icons – *murtis* – to which they directed their worship. These *murtis*, made of clay, wood, brick, stone and other materials, were housed in shrines – roofed enclosures of thatch, mud, wood and brick were built. These shrines enabled villagers to gather for collective public worship. Most of these shrines were of a temporary nature, erected for special ceremonial occasions. Others were built for more long term use to protect the *murtis* and other sacred objects.

EARLY EVIDENCE

Textual, archaeological and epigraphic evidence reveal the

Facing page:
Early cave mandir at
Badami, Karnataka

existence of worship places housing deities from at least the fourth century BCE. Panini's *Ashtadhyayi*, Kautilya's *Arthashastra* as well as Buddhist and Jain texts describe such structures. Excavations at Gudimallam in Andhra Pradesh have unearthed structures that sheltered icons of Hindu deities. Other archaeological discoveries demonstrate that shrines dedicated to several deities have existed in some parts of India since at least the 2nd to 1st century BCE; for example, the shrines at Besnagar, near Vidisha in Madhya Pradesh (2nd century BCE), Nagari in the Chittor district of Andhra Pradesh (1st century BCE) and Atranjikhera in the Etah district of Uttar Pradesh (c. 2nd-1st century BCE).[i]

Further evidence of Hindu shrines is found on coins from this early era. A 2nd-1st century BCE square copper coin of the Audumbaras of Punjab shows a shrine with a double roof level supported by pillars (see top figure in left margin).[ii] Epigraphic proof includes a 131 BCE inscription referring to a pillar erected in honour of Vasudev and an inscription at Nandsa in Udaipur district, referring to a Vedic sacrifice performed after building shrines to Brahma, Indra, Prajapati and Vishnu.

Naturally, the use of wood, clay and other easily perishable materials has meant that these shrines have not endured the vagaries of time and climate. Consequently, the paucity of physical and textual evidence hampers a full understanding of the development of mandirs. However, the available evidence indicates that later mandirs are a development from these early practices.

Over the past two centuries scholars have diligently studied thousands of mandirs and analyzed architectural, textual, geographic, cultural, historical, political, linguistic, spiritual and other factors and charted the development of mandir architecture throughout India over many centuries.

EARLY STYLES

From the early centuries CE mandirs were built of more durable materials, such as, bricks and stones. Also, from around the 2nd century BCE, rock-cut architecture began and continued for over a thousand years. Rock-cut mandirs differ from the structural type in that the building is carved out of the rock instead of being assembled. Thus, the caves are excavations, cut out of the rock and

2nd-1st century BCE copper coin with a double-roof shrine engraving

Illustration of Vedic era enclosure for rituals and murtis

i. Ray, H.P. (2004) 'The Apsidal Shrine in Early Hinduism: Origins, Cultic Affiliation, Patronage', *World Archaeology*, Vol. 36, No. 3, pp. 343-359.
ii. Ray, H.P. (2009) 'The Shrine in Early Hinduism: The Changing Sacred Landscape', *The Journal of Hindu Studies*, Vol. 2, No. 1, pp. 76-96.

Kailas Mandir at
Ellora Caves,
Maharashtra

created by a method of subtraction. So, even though architectural terminology is used to describe them, they are basically more like sculpture than architecture, since the pillars, beams and other architectural elements are sculpted from the rock.

The earliest use of caves for carving out places of worship was by Buddhists and Jains. The oldest surviving rock-cut caves in India are the Barabar Caves in Bihar, built during the Maurya period. Hindus produced cave mandirs at a later time, of which the caves at Badami, Elephanta and Ellora are excellent examples. The coexistence of structures from three different religions in the same locality is a splendid representation of the religious tolerance of India since ancient times.

The architectural and decorative designs of later stone mandirs originated in the early wood and thatch buildings and have persisted for centuries in the stone structures. It is the remnants of these extant stone and rock structures built over many centuries that help to chart the development of mandir architecture. These mandirs encapsulate a profound tradition and demonstrate the outstanding creativity and craftsmanship of the artisans. They represent the heart and soul of India, and the story of their development provides an intriguing insight into the spiritual mind of Hindus.

6

Varieties of Mandir Structure

This chapter provides a glimpse into some of the regional styles of mandirs that evolved in different parts of India.

The early mandir forms, built of perishable materials, served as models upon which later stone mandirs were built and developed.

SOUTH INDIA

South India includes the present-day states of Tamil Nadu, Kerala, Andhra Pradesh and Karnataka. The ruling dynasties of each region guided the development of mandirs in their territory.

In Tamil Nadu, under the patronage of the Pallava dynasty in the 7th century, the earliest mandirs were of the rock-cut variety. Among the most well-known are the rock-cut mandirs on the coast at Mahabalipuram. There are monolithic and structural mandirs and represent the early phases of the *dravida* mandir style.

Carved from large rocks, the mandirs are called *rathas*, a term which signifies both a form of mandir and a wooden chariot. The *rathas* comprise of single or multiple cellas with a pillared veranda or hall. They are decorated with *dravida*-style architectural elements.

Also at Mahabalipuram is the famous 8th century Shore Mandir, which is one of the earliest structural mandirs in South India. Thereafter, construction of structural mandirs flourished, mainly in the *dravida* and *vesara* styles. However, some *nagara* style mandirs were also built in this region.

Incorporating features of both the *nagara* and *dravida* styles, the main characteristics of the *vesara* style are a sanctum with a pyramidal roof, pillared halls, passages with sloping roofs circling

From humble beginnings, the mandir structure has developed into an architectural marvel. From north to south and east to west, India is blessed with an abundant variety of breathtaking mandirs.

Facing page:
Kandariya Mahadev at Khajuraho, Madhya Pradesh

Ratha mandirs at Mahabalipuram, Tamil Nadu

the sanctum, porches and perforated stone screens.

The *dravida* style has three defining characteristics: recessed sculptures, tiered *shikhars* and gopurams. The square sanctum is topped by a pyramidal *shikhar* comprising of multiple receding storeys, creating a strong visual of horizontal lines. The sanctum is surrounded by columned halls and all significant structures are crowned by a dome, which can be square, round, apsidal, octagonal or oblong (barrel) in shape. *Dravida* sculptures are recessed into the walls and offset by pilasters.

The *dravida* mandir complex is enclosed by one or more concentric walls with a *gopuram* in the middle of each wall. As the number of concentric walls increased, the *gopurams* increased in height the further their distance from the main shrine. Thus, the sanctum of the main deity was no longer the tallest structure in the mandir complex. However, the sanctity of the *shikhar* remained undiminished.

These two styles (*dravida* and *vesara*) developed in two periods: first, from the 6th century CE to the 12th century and then from the 13th to 17th centuries. In the first period, the emphasis was on the mandir plan, design and elevation of the architectural elements. In the second period, the focus shifted to horizontal expansion,

Pattadakal, Karnataka: To the left is the dravida-style Mallikarjuna Mandir. On the right is the *nagara*-style Kashivisvanath Mandir

with development of secondary structures to cater for personal and collective worship rituals and celebration of festivals.

In South India, some locations are a rich repository of mandirs reflecting how the styles evolved through the medieval period.

Pattadakal

Together with Aihole and Badami, Pattadakal has excellent mandirs built by the Chalukyas in the 7th and 8th centuries. The Virupaksha and Mallikarjuna mandirs represent the pinnacle of Chalukya architecture.

The now ruined 7th century Galaganatha Mandir, dedicated to Lord Shiva, is based on a *nagara* plan, but resembles the *vesara* style in its structure. The Sangameshvara Mandir follows the *vesara* style. The Kashivishvanatha Mandir combines *dravida* architectural elements with a *nagara shikhar*.

In the 9th and 10th centuries, the Rashtrakuta dynasty added to the mandirs here.

Thanjavur

With their capital at Thanjavur, the Chola dynasty kings built grand structural mandirs. The mandirs at Thanjavur (1010 CE)

Meenakshi Mandir complex,
Madurai, Tamil Nadu

and Gangaikondacholapuram (1025 CE) are of immense size and impresssive quality. The mandirs feature high *vimanas, gopurams,* enclosure walls, long *mandaps* and excellent sculptures.

Hampi (Vijayanagara)

Hampi, also known as Vijayanagara, was the capital of the Vijayanagara dynasty. The mandirs predating Vijayanagara rule (8th to 13th century) are mainly located in the surrounding hills. They are mainly *vesara* in style, but have a *dravida* style superstructure. There are also some *nagara* style shrines, built between the 10th and 14th centuries.

Mandir development in the Vijayanagara era can be divided into three phases. In the first (1336-1404) and second (1405-1485) phases, the mandirs were of limited size and embellishment. The third phase (1486-1570) set the framework for future structural developments.

Elaborate ornamentation of ceilings, boundary walls (*prakaras*) with large ornate *gopurams* on two sides, a circumambulatory path, large *mandaps* and multiple secondary shrines were the main

features of this style. The Virupaksha Mandir represents a typical example of this style.

Madurai

The Meenakshi Mandir in Madurai, Tamil Nadu, was initially built by the Pandya dynasty. Subsequently, restorations and expansions were carried out by the Vijayanagara and Nayaka rulers.

The mandir has a twin shrine, huge pillared halls, towering gates and a large water tank.

Thus, in South India, while preserving the basic *dravida* features, local variations have enriched the mandir architecture.

CENTRAL INDIA

This region includes the states of Maharashtra, Madhya Pradesh and Chhatisgarh. It also includes part of the Deccan Plateau.

Examples of rock-cut mandirs are found at Elephanta and Ellora.

The earliest built Hindu mandirs in India are located in this region. They are small rectangular shrines, some of which are raised on plinths and some have porches.

Chennakeshava Mandir,
Belur, Karnataka

Lathe-turned type pillar,
characteristic of the
Hoysala dynasty

Khajuraho is an important site where about twenty-five Hindu and Jain mandirs, built between the 9th and 12th centuries, have been well preserved. The main Hindu mandirs are the Kandariya Mahadev, Lakshmana and Vishvanatha. They are built on high terraces and accessed by stairs at the front. The mandirs also have a circumambulatory path. The *shikhars* of the *ardhamandap, mahamandap* and *garbhagruha* gradually increase in vertical height to give a mountainous appearance to each mandir.

The number of wall projections also increased, resulting in more vertical lines and so adding to the vertical emphasis.

In the Deccan are mandirs built by the Hoysala dynasty (11th to 14th centuries). Also known as Dvarasamudra, Halebid was the capital of the Hoysala dynasty. The mandir here is representative of the Hoysala style. The mandir is a large double-shrined (*dvikuta*) *dravida vimana*, based on a *pancharatha* plan. There are two open halls with 'lathe-turned' pillars. There are eight sculpted friezes on the base and sculptures of Hindu deities and scriptural scenes on the walls. The *antarala* (vestibule) also has decorative ceilings.

WESTERN INDIA

Medieval *nagara* mandir styles are categorized into four main

regional varieties: eastern, central, northern (upper India) and western.

The distinctive feature of *nagara* mandirs is the vertical emphasis of the *shikhar* (superstructure), in contrast to the horizontal, layered sections of *dravida* superstructures.

In both the *dravida* and *nagara* styles, a *kalash* is placed on top of the crown to indicate that the mandir has been ritually consecrated.

An impressive array of artistic innovations was adopted to give each region a unique style. In later *nagara* mandirs, domes were also added. Due to its wide geographical spread, the *nagara* style has many regional variations implemented by the ruling dynasties.

Beginning from around the 7th century, in the present-day states of Gujarat and Rajasthan, the western variety, also known as the Maru-Gurjara style, was of the longest duration and most prolific.

Preceding this style were the Maha-Maru style of Rajasthan, Maha-Gurjara style of north Gujarat and the Surashtra style of south Saurashtra.

The geographical extent of these mandir styles is from Parnagar in Barmer district, Rajasthan, in the north to Parol near Mumbai in the south, and from Osian and Kiradu in the west to Atru in the east.

The earliest extant mandir in this region is the late 6th century CE

Mukteshwar Mandir,
Bhuvaneshwar, Orissa

mandir at Gop in the Barda Hill region of southwest Saurashtra (see photo on p. 92). It is built on a high podium and is tall rectangulr tower structure with closed *gavakshas*.

The Maha-Maru style mandirs are usually built on a platform and have walls decorated with sculptures of deities and other celestial beings, tall pediments, *shikhars* with a lattice of creepers, and pilasters decorated with vase and foliage designs and carved panels. For example, the Harihara Mandir at Osian.

Mandirs of the Maha-Gurjara style are relatively plain compared to Maha-Maru mandirs. They have plain walls, no preceding hall and a *phamsana* (stepped pyramid) roof. The mandirs at Roda in Gujarat represent this style.

In the 11th century, the Maha-Maru and Maha-Gurjara styles combined to form the Maru-Gurjara style which became prevalent throughout Gujarat and Rajasthan. The style is identified by the arrangement and intricate decoration of its constituent elements. The Surya Mandir at Modhera, built by the Solanki dynasty, is a fine example of the Maru-Gurjara style.

EAST INDIA

This region includes the present-day states of Orissa, Bengal

and Bihar. The early period of mandir building here is marked by much experimentation.

Dedicated to Shiva, the Mundeshvari Mandir at Ramgarh in Bihar was built in the early 7th century. Its interior has four pillars which support a flat ceiling, though the roof has now collapsed.

From about the early 7th century, the uniform ground plan and curvilinear *shikhar* of the *nagara* style was introduced. Thereafter, regional variations evolved based on these core features.

In Bihar, the *triratha* ground plan emerged, resulting in three staggered wall segments. This evolved into walls with five (*pancharatha*) and seven (*saptaratha*) segments.

In later years, a horizontal layer separated the staggered wall segments in half between its *vedibandha* (base) and entablature, and balconied windows were added to the *mahamandap*. This is seen in the ruined remains of the Shiva Mandir at Umga.

Mandirs in Bengal were initially *triratha* in plan, with the walls divided into three sections vertically. They had *shikhars* divided into *bhumis* (horizontal sections) by *bhumi-amalaks* and topped by a flat *amalak*.

In Jharkhand also, *nagara* style mandirs were built on a *triratha* plan. The *shikhar* was divided into horizontal sections

Surya Mandir,
Konark, Orissa

by ribbed, right-angled *bhumi-amalaks* and crowned by a large flat, spheroid *amalak*. For example, the Durga Mandir at Diari and Mahishasuramardini Mandir at Haradih.

Later mandirs had more mouldings in the *vedibandha* and pilasters on the outermost *ratha* segment of the wall. After a period of development, there was a decline in the architectural intricacy of the style in this region.

In Orissa, the *deul* (local word for the sanctum) was, in the early phase, *triratha* in plan with upto four mouldings in the *vedibandha* (locally called *pabhaga*) and niches in the vertical face of each wall segment (*ratha*). The curvilinear *shikhar* was divided by *bhumi-amalaks* and had a *beki* (short cylindrical neck), a flat *amalak*, a low *khapuri* (skull-like element) and cylindrical *kalash* at the top. Later, a *mahamandap* was added.

In the transitional phase in Orissa, the *deul* was built on a *pancharatha* plan, the number of mouldings on the *vedibandha* increased, and most significantly, a pyramidal roof with gradually receding tiers was added to the *mahamandap*. The small Mukteshwar Mandir in Bhuvaneshwar best represents this phase and is considered a gem of Orissan architecture.

In the mature phase, the *deul* was *pancharatha* in ground plan,

Ruined remains of the
Surya Mandir at Martand,
Jammu and Kashmir

the wall (called *bara*) had five vertical divisions and the *shikhar* was almost perpendicular. Some mandirs added a *natya mandap* (dancing hall) and a *bhogamandap* (hall for offerings), all enclosed by an outer wall. The Orissa style is characterized by its general astylar construction – a plain interior without pillars and a lavishly decorated exterior.

The Lingaraja Mandir (1115 CE) in Bhuvaneshwar is an outstanding example of the mature phase. The Surya Mandir in Konark represents the pinnacle of Orissan mandir architecture.

NORTH INDIA

Of the very few mandirs of the early period in this region which are extant, the mandir at Bhitargaon in Uttar Pradesh was built in the Gupta period and is dated to the 5th century CE. It is a brick shrine built on a high terrace with a pyramidal *shikhar* and has terracota sculpture decorations in niches on the exterior.

In Kashmir, is the now-ruined 8th century CE Surya Mandir at Martand, remnants of 9th century mandirs at Avantipur and the 12th century Shiva Mandir at Pandrethan.

Due to the extreme weather conditions in this region, overhanging eaves are common, as are pagoda-type *shikhars*.

7

Patronage, Guilds and Mandir Economy

PATRONAGE

Many shastras describe that sponsoring the construction of mandirs is given considerable importance and earns great spiritual merit.

"Let him who wishes to enter the worlds that are reached by sacrificial offerings and the performance of religious obligations build a mandir to the gods, by doing which he attains both the results of sacrifice and the performance of religious obligations" (*Bruhatsamhita*, LV:2).

The *Shilpaprakasha* assures that the patron "will always have peace, wealth, grain and sons".

The *Vishnu Dharmottara Puran* states that the donor of the land for building a mandir attains the abode of the particular deity of that mandir.

Ancient inscriptions reveal that, at first, it was mainly ordinary people – farmers, merchants, craftsmen's guilds, housewives, monks, nuns and others – who sponsored the building of mandirs. Kings would give indirect support for the subsistence of religious places, even of faiths other than their own.

However, during medieval times, a distinct change occurred. Whereas previously, rulers had not directly patronized places of worship, even those of deities whom they personally worshipped, inscriptions show that kings, queens and other royals had started

Facing page:
Artisans at work in a
workshop in Rajasthan

to directly sponsor such monuments. Donations from royal patrons and private individuals were received by the mandir in the form of money, valuable objects, livestock or income from grants of land, including whole villages. Grants not only financed the building of mandirs but also provided for their upkeep, renovation and the performance of rituals.

Donors gave grants to a mandir wishing for religious merit and to earn ultimate *moksha*. Hindus believe that whatever wealth they have is given by God and should be used in such good works. Thus, through patronage of religious places, royals and other public figures fulfilled this obligation and, at the same time, enhanced their social reputations.

This tradition existed for many centuries and resulted in thousands of mandirs of varying sizes and designs scattered throughout the whole of India. These mandirs were expressions of the deep-rooted faith of the monarchs and at the same time nurtured the faith of the citizens.

However, as the political set up of India changed and dynastic rule subsided, the nature of mandir funding changed. What was previously considered the responsibility of wealthy rulers reverted to and was admirably undertaken by ordinary citizens – generally people of modest or little means. Thus, the task of building and maintaining mandirs became the collective responsibility of the people. That this responsibility has been ably shouldered by the ordinary people is a powerful reflection of their faith in God.

Today, even as the 21st century brings in widespread changes to life everywhere on earth, the building of mandirs continues. Hindu communities, in India and wherever they are anywhere on the globe, gather to set up mandirs in their locality. They may not be like the majestic architectural masterpieces of the past, though some are, but they certainly represent their firm faith in God and their affiliation for Hindu values and worship.

MANDIR ECONOMY

As mandirs became wealthy they could afford to become employers and act as patrons. Improvements in agriculture were also embarked upon by the mandir, with provision of such facilities as water tanks, canals and new roads. So, by providing employment to artisans, peasants and shepherds mandirs played an important role in redistributing wealth to other segments of society.

As mandirs provided work and the means of livelihood for a

large number of persons, they were able to exert great influence upon the economic life of the community.

Even small mandirs needed the services of priests, garland-makers and suppliers of clarified butter, milk and oil. One of the most detailed accounts that has been preserved on the number of people who were supported by a mandir, and the wages they received, is that given in an inscription on the Bruhadeshvar Mandir at Thanjavur dated to 1011 CE. The list includes dancing masters, dance performers, singers, pipers, drummers, lute players, conch blowers, mandir superintendents, women musicians, accountants, sacred parasol bearers, lamp lighters, water sprinklers, potters, washermen, astrologers, tailors, jewellers, brazier lighters, carpenters and goldsmith supervisors, all totalling more than six hundred people. Most of the employees rendering these services worked part-time as payment was in land, which they had to cultivate.

There are also instances of hospitals associated with mandirs where beds were provided for the sick. Feeding houses were established in which free food was provided daily to the poor and needy.

The mandir has always been a centre of intellectual and artistic life for the Hindu community, functioning not only as a place of worship, but also as a nucleus for cultural activities. Within the mandir, subjects such as grammar and astrology were taught as well as the recital and analysis of sacred texts. Endowments to mandirs were made specifically for the establishment of colleges which were incorporated into mandir complexes. Some mandirs would house a number of residential students in boarding schools attached to the mandir.

Music and dance generally formed part of the daily ritual of the mandir and during special celebrations and annual festivals these played a particularly dominant role. Large mandirs would maintain their own musicians, both vocal and instrumental, together with dancers, actors and teachers of the performing arts.

Such activities led to increased administrative work and the requirement for more mandir staff and buildings to facilitate the activities. In this way, in addition to their pivotal function as centres of religious worship, mandirs evolved into a vast, extensive complex encompassing many roles to serve the spiritual, social, cultural and secular needs of society.

Artisans draw the the design to be carved on the stone before they begin sculpturing

EXPERT ARTISANS

Although the financing of mandir construction necessitated patrons, the actual construction was effected by architects and craftsmen. Before the advent and adoption of modern building codes and methodologies, mandir construction in the classical Indian tradition was carried out by four categories of experts: *sthapati, sutragrahin, vardhaki* and *takshak*. In addition to having the special skills of his category, each individual was expected to be calm and of pure character. These craftsmen carried out the instructions of the *sthapak*, the architect-priest, who has the qualification of an *acharya*. The *Shilparatna* (I. 29-42) says of the *sthapak*:

"He who wishes to build villages, royal palaces, tanks, or mandirs, should select a *sthapak* and *shilpi* for the purpose. Let the *sthapak* be a Brahmin who knows the meaning of the sacred texts, the Vedas and Agamas, and who observes the rules of conduct according to his caste (*varna*) and stage of life (*ashram*), who has received initiation (*diksha*), is competent, dedicates himself to his work and is a believer (*astik*) in the sacred tradition."

The *sthapati*, the chief architect, was very pious, knowledgeable in the shastras, and had the overall responsibility for planning,

Group of craftsmen in a workshop sculpting a dome for Swaminarayan Akshardham, New Delhi

designing and coordinating all aspects of the construction from start to finish and rendering the initial vision into the final masterpiece.

The *sutragrahin* was like a chief engineer or surveyor. He was the supervisor and was normally the *sthapati's* son or senior assistant. He was also proficient in the shastras and an expert draftsman, who supervised the other craftsmen according to the instructions of the *sthapati* to ensure that all building elements were arranged appropriately.

The *takshak* was the sculptor who produced the magnificent carvings and was also responsible for all the intricate woodwork for doors, windows, pillars, etc.

The *vardhaki* was the stonemason, plasterer, painter or other craftsman who pieced together the building elements sculpted by the *takshak*.

In addition to this primary group of specialists, various supportive functions were also carried out by other people. Women were employed for lighter work such as cleaning and polishing stones. There were workmen for every skill: stonemasons to cut stones to size, artisans to fashion them into architectural forms, and sculptors to do the finest chisel work. Specialists carried out particular jobs such as laying out the axes of the building, grinding the polishing

Craftsmen apply the finishing touches to the sculpture of a narrative scene on the Gajendra Pith at Swaminarayan Akshardham, New Delhi

materials, carving the bands of friezes and mixing the coloured pigments for paintwork.

Brahmins performed various rituals at every important stage of work, such as, the purification of the site, the initial tracing of the ground plan, the foundation stone-laying ceremony, placing of the first pillar, the setting of the crowning finial of the superstructure, and the consecration of the *murti* of the deity in the inner sanctum. With such established organization, the genius of the Indian craftsmen came to the fore.

GUILDS

By the 7th century CE, craftsmen had formed guilds to ensure preservation of their special knowledge and skills, to secure better working conditions, and to guarantee a minimum standard of workmanship quality. The guilds had considerabe influence over mandir construction. Guilds had judicial rights over their own members and could expel a rebellious member.

Within the guilds, traditional knowledge and skills were usually passed on from generation to generation in which sons were taught by their fathers during a long apprenticeship. This transmission of knowledge and skills was often the main inheritance given by the

प्रासादा वीतरागस्य पुरमध्ये सुखावहाः ।
गुरुकल्याणकर्तारश्चतुर्दिक्षु प्रकल्पयेत् ॥

स्वशक्त्येष्टकमृत्काष्ठशैलधातुजरत्नजम् ।
देवतायतनं कुर्याद् धर्मार्थकाममोक्षदम् ॥

तूणैः कोटिगुणं पुण्यं मृन्मये दशधा ततः ।
इष्टकाभिः शतं तस्मात् शैलेयेऽनन्तकं स्मृतम् ॥

प्रासादानाञ्च सर्वेषां जायते दशभेदता ।
चतुर्दश प्रवर्तन्ते ज्ञेया लोकानुसारतः ॥

ज्ञात्वा लक्षणलक्ष्याणि गुरुमार्गानुसारतः ।
प्रासादभवनादीनां सर्वं ज्ञानमवाप्नुयात् ॥

शुभलग्ने सुनक्षत्रे पञ्चग्रहबलान्विते ।
माससंक्रान्तिवत्सादिनिषिद्धकालवर्जिते ॥

रात्रौ दिक्साधनं कुर्याद् दीपसूत्रध्रुवैक्यतः ।
रमे भूमिप्रदेशे तु शङ्कुना दिवसे तथा ॥

हस्तमात्रं खनेद् भूमिं मृत्तिकाञ्च विपूरयेत् ।
उद्धृता च समा न्यूना श्रेष्ठमध्यकनिष्ठिका ॥

तत्सर्वं समाशोध्य जलेन परिपूरयेत् ।
शिल्पी आत्मनां मत्वा जलं पुण्येत्यगावत ॥

पाते कोटिगुणा ज्येषा कथिता व्याहृतानके ।
सम्पूर्ण राफला भूमिः सर्वकार्यार्थसाधिनी ॥

Artisans at work in a workshop and on site

father to his sons, who, in turn, continued the tradition. As the means of livelihood of these families depended on their knowledge and skill, tradition and techniques were often carefully guarded.

Mandir building projects of large magnitude often took more than one generation of craftsmen to finish. So groups of artisans would reside near the building sites for many years, where young men learnt from their seniors.

Members of guilds also frequently travelled from one region to another in order to work on different projects, accounting for much of the spread of architectural and artistic traditions that took place throughout the history of the mandir's development. Over time, distinct schools of art and architecture developed based on the *nagara* style – e.g., Orissan, Chalukyan, Gujarati, Kashmiri and others – and the *dravida* style. Despite the variations, the *vastushastras* gave a certain amount of uniformity to the constructions.

Guilds frequently became wealthy and powerful and there are many inscriptions recording their charitable donations.

8

Textual Basis of Mandirs

The *vastushastras* are sacred texts on Hindu art and architecture. They include *sthapatya* shastras, which mainly describe mandir architecture, and the *shilpa* shastras, which focus on art and sculpture.

In practice, mandir architecture and sculpture are inseparable, since sculptures are integral to a mandir's structure.

The earliest application of *vastushastras* was in the construction of ceremonial altars for Vedic rituals. The structures for these altars were calculated and designed on the basis of Vedic geometry from the *Shulbasutras*.

Later, as mandir building became more widespread, the master-builders transmitted much of their technical knowledge to their pupils orally. So, they did not write down all the details, such as their methods of construction, polishing and dressing stones, or transporting stones to great heights. These techniques were taught during the practical training every architect had to undergo under the guidance of his teacher.

Only in early medieval times, around the 6th century CE, did written documentation of this information begin in earnest. The treatises themselves are theoretical guides written by learned Brahmins, who were mainly concerned that theological and spiritual aspects of the mandir structure were strictly adhered to, thus qualifying a mandir as a mandir. Even then, in general, the *vastushastras* were committed to memory and passed down the generations after learning them by heart.

There is overlap of content and differences in level of details provided in the various *shilpa* and *sthapatya* texts. These shastras contain the various rules that establish standards for designing and constructing mandirs and other buildings. They deal with such topics as site selection, soil testing, building materials and techniques, design of mandirs, images, palaces, dwellings and gates, and town planning. They also indicate the skills required by the architect and other artisans involved in the process and the work to be carried out by each.

The shastras are a guide for building secular as well as sacred buildings, and contain material on the layout of cities, forts and military settlements.

The texts also helped to ensure that a certain quality would always be achieved by following the rules they contained. However, despite the exactness of the regulations, the texts permitted tremendous flexibility in practice such that there are an inexhaustible variety of mandir designs.

Despite such detailed descriptions, some of the extant texts are incomplete in content, since, for ancient authors certain ideas and practices were so ingrained and natural that they have omitted them from the texts.

It is possible that the texts were compiled and written after construction to document the process rather than as a detailed guide for use on site. Hence, there are some difficulties in following the flow of the texts. For example, treatises do not adequately explain the precise role of the *vastupurush mandala* in generating mandir plans and the relation of a structure's elevation to its plan is also not systematically explained. In addition, the lack of diagrams in the texts to visually clarify and elaborate upon the written details makes understanding more difficult.

Also, over the years, additions have been made to the texts, further complicating the task of dating and understanding them. Thus, an expert, or guru, is essential to properly comprehend them and apply their teachings. The texts seem to have been used by those involved in the building process – patron, priest, architects and others – according to their role in the process. Therefore, inexperienced readers are likely to interpret the details inaccurately.

Naturally, the contents of texts varied regionally, with different texts becoming more accepted and established as the standard texts in north, south and east India.

As a result, modern scholars differ in their opinions regarding how strictly mandirs were built in accordance with the *vastushastra* texts. It is natural that, due to unfamiliarity with the ancient language and changes in modern technical requirements and equipment, the texts are less used today as a basis for mandir building.

THE VASTU LITERATURE

Among the *vastushastra* texts are *Manasara*, which describes the principles of architectural and sculptural construction. *Mayamatam* of Maya is a rich South Indian text with 36 chapters, beginning with the selection of a site for construction, and describing different ways of construction. *Vishwakarma Prakash* also deals with the same subjects from a different angle, while *Samarangana Sutradhara*, by King Bhoja of Malwa (1018-1060 CE), contains descriptions on house construction, town planning and mandir architecture.

Some of the more important and established *vastu* texts include: *Aparajitapriccha, Bruhatsamhita, Mayamatam, Manasara, Vishwakarma Prakash, Samaranganasutradhara, Rajavallabha, Manasollasa, Vaikhanasagama, Kamikagama, Vastuvidhya, Shilparatna, Aitareya Brahmana, Apastamba Srauta Sutra, Kashyapashilpa, Shilpaprakasha, Vishwakarma Vastu Shastra, Vayu Puran, Vishudharmottara Puran, Agni Puran, Skanda Puran, Garuda Puran, Bhavishya Puran, Mandana Sutradhar* and *Deeparnava*.

9

Site Selection and Preparation

SITE SELECTION

"The gods always play where groves, rivers, mountains and springs are near, and in towns with pleasure gardens" (*Bruhatsamhita, LV. 4-8; Bhavisya Puran, I. CXXX. 11-15*).

It is not surprising, then, that many of India's ancient mandirs have been built in lush valleys or groves, where the environment is thought to be particularly suitable for building a residence for the gods.

Indian architecture texts describe the selection of a site for building a mandir. The *Bruhatsamhita,* written by the famous sage-scientist Varahamihir, lists forests, places lush with greenery, confluences of rivers and mountains as ideal places to worship God. The *Vishnudharmottara Puran* suggests setting up mandirs on holy grounds, river banks, caves and mountain summits where natural purity is in abundance. Places where water is freely available are considered excellent. So, ideally, spots of natural beauty are chosen as mandir sites. Obviously, this is not hard and fast as circumstances and populations will also be an important factor in determining where a mandir should be built.

In ancient India, mandirs were generally centred around *tirths* – places of pilgrimage – since they help the spiritual seeker walk the path of liberation due to their inherent purity.

Tirths were generally found on riverbanks or ocean shores, where water was plentiful. Due to its purity, water was given an important role, being used in rituals and worship by devotees. The rivers and

"The gods always play where groves, rivers, mountains and springs are near, and in towns with pleasure gardens."
- Bruhatsamhita, Bhavisya Puran

Facing page:
Bhutanatha Group of Mandirs, Badami, Karnataka

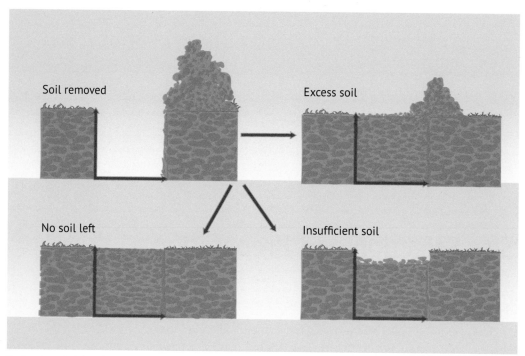

Soil removed

Excess soil

No soil left

Insufficient soil

Testing the suitability of a site by removing soil to produce a pit and refilling it with the excavated soil

oceans themselves were often offered oblations, their water being treated with reverence. Flowers or plants growing in water were also considered as symbolizing spiritual purity – in particular the lotus flower was given importance as being a symbol of freshness and spiritual enlightenment. Thus, places near natural water were given first preference when choosing sites for mandir construction.

Even for worship and sacred rites, water is an integral part of the ceremonies. So, if no natural water was available, artificial lakes, wells or water tanks were created for that purpose.

The same importance is given to trees and plants. Places where these are plentiful are highly recommended for mandir building.

TESTING SITE SUITABILITY

To determine the suitability of the land certain tests were devised, as described below.

A hole of 2 ft. × 2 ft. × 2 ft. was dug and the soil removed was again used to refill the hole. If some soil remained after refilling then the land was considered well suited for mandir building. If no soil was left then the land was of average quality. If there was a shortage of soil then the land was regarded as unsuitable.

In another test, a 2 ft. × 2 ft. × 2 ft. hole was filled with water

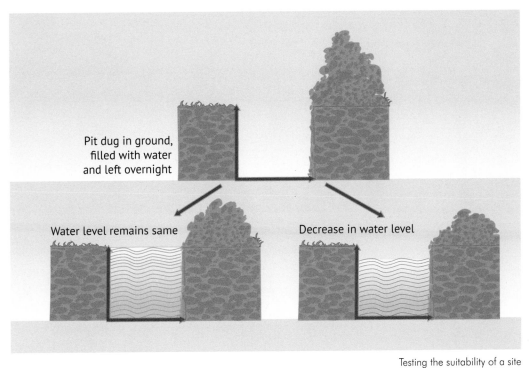

Pit dug in ground,
filled with water
and left overnight

Water level remains same

Decrease in water level

Testing the suitability of a site
by digging a pit and filling it
with water to see how much
remains the next morning

at night and the next morning the amount of water remaining indicated the land quality. If the hole remained full of water the land was judged to be of good quality for building. If the water level was reduced then the land was regarded as inappropriate for construction.

The strength of the foundation is dependent on the strength of the land. To test the loadbearing capacity of the land its porosity is tested. If the porosity is low then the density is high; consequently its strength is high and therefore its loadbearing capacity is high.

If high density and low porosity soil is dug up and the same soil is used to fill up the hole then excess soil remains; such land is regarded as good for constructing a building such as a mandir. If low porosity soil is filled with water then it is not absorbed quickly. Therefore, from the land's water absorption rate one can determine the strength of the land. From this we can see how scientific the ancient techniques were.

These and other practical tests are described in the *Bruhat-samhita* and other texts. Other factors about the soil which were considered include its sound, smell, shape, consistency, colour and fertility.

SITE PURIFICATION

Scriptures also say that the land to be used for the mandir site should be pure. Two types of purity – physical and metaphysical – need to be achieved. Physical cleansing involves removal of any extraneous matter, such as, the remains of dead creatures or impure objects, such as, bone. Details are provided in various texts.

Metaphysical cleansing involves ridding the earth of unseen evil elements and subtle impurities via the process of chanting strength-evoking mantras. Hinduism's ancient and wise sages were of the opinion that contact of wicked individuals or unhealthy thoughts can be detrimental to the environment.

As far as possible, a mandir should be constructed without breaking the delicate laws and rhythms of nature. It is imperative that at proposed mandir sites, care is taken so that the harm to wildlife, birds, insects and trees is minimized. To what extent? The scriptures say that if a tree has to be cut, a prayer for its next birth should be uttered. The text *Apstamba Shrautsutra* goes as far as to say that one should request the axe cutting a tree, "Chop this tree in such a way that it inflicts as little pain as possible on the tree."

INITIAL SITE PREPARATION

After the ground has been chosen with due regard to its qualities, the *sthapati* arranges an auspicious time for the purification rites (*bhumipujan*), offering of the appropriate oblations and for consecrated water and flowers to be sprinkled throughout the site, accompanied with invocations for the prosperity of the builder. The soil is then ploughed, after performing certain ceremonies prescribed for this occasion. The implements to be used, such as, axe, spade, stone-cutters, chisels, carpenters tools, etc. are also offered puja.

When the ground is tilled and ploughed, the past ceases to count; new life is entrusted to the soil and another cycle of production begins, an assurance that the rhythm of nature has not been interfered with. The trees and bushes are removed while auspicious mantras are chanted. These rituals are significant as they seek the permission of the flora to be removed, indicating the great reverence to nature in ancient times. After these rites the ground is levelled, indicating that order has been established in a wild, unruly and errant world.

After the earth has been ploughed, tilled and levelled, the *vastupurush mandala*, the metaphysical plan of the mandir, is drawn.

Facing page:
Pramukh Swami Maharaj performs the bhumipujan of the Swaminarayan Akshardham, New Delhi, site. Then, the foundations are excavated and prepared using modern techniques and technology,.

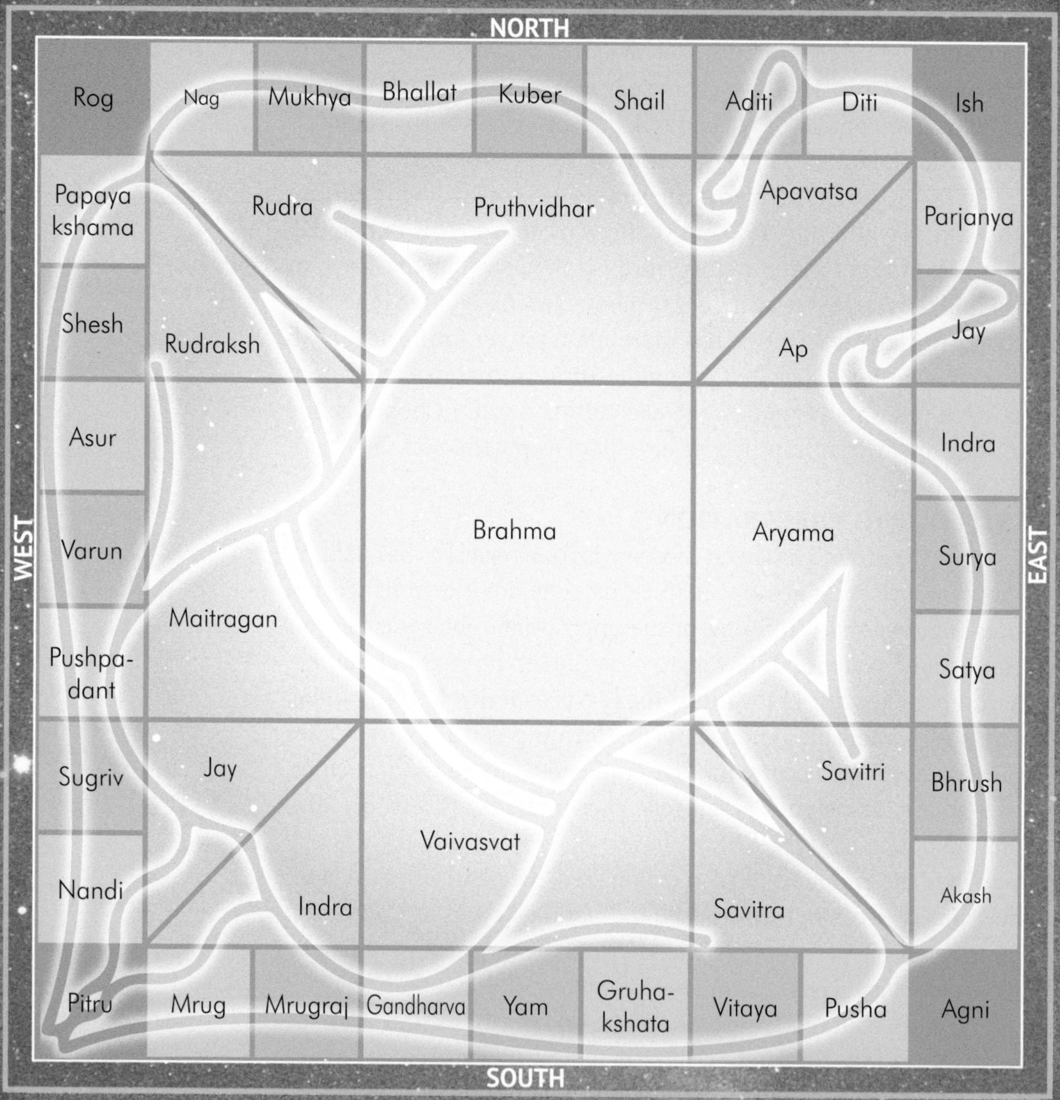
NORTH
Rog
Nag
Mukhya
Bhallat
Kuber
Shail
Aditi
Diti
Ish
Papaya kshama
Rudra
Pruthvidhar
Apavatsa
Parjanya
Shesh
Rudraksh
Ap
Jay
Asur
Indra
WEST
Varun
Brahma
Aryama
Surya
EAST
Maitragan
Pushpa-dant
Satya
Sugriv
Jay
Savitri
Bhrush
Vaivasvat
Nandi
Indra
Savitra
Akash
Pitru
Mrug
Mrugraj
Gandharva
Yam
Gruha-kshata
Vitaya
Pusha
Agni
SOUTH

10

Vastupurush Mandala

The *vastupurush mandala* is an essential component of the Vastushastra, providing the mathematical and diagrammatic basis for preparing building designs. *Vastu* means the physical dwelling; *purush* is the cosmic man; and *mandala* is the common name for any plan or design and symbolizes the cosmos.

The story describing the origin of the Vastupurush or "the spirit of the site" is found in the Purans, e.g., Matsya Puran, and several Indian architectural texts.

The most common version is as follows: Shiva was engaged in a duel with a demon named Andhaka, an evil spirit who was born from the drops of Shiva's sweat. This spirit had a terrifying appearance and insatiable hunger. By performing great austerities, the spirit won a boon from Shiva that allowed him to swallow the three worlds: Swarg, Mrutyulok and Patal. As this spirit stretched and began to occupy the heavens, he fell flat on the earth. At this time 45 gods and divine spirits seized the opportunity and pinned various parts of the spirit's body to the ground, rendering him helpless. This spirit came to be called Vastupurush because the gods had lodged themselves on his body. The deities, in pinning him down, occupied different parts of his body and continued to reside there. In order to satisfy his hunger, the deity, Brahma, ordained that the spirit receive offerings from people on building sites before construction. Also, since his body is spread out over the ground, with his head at the northeast corner and feet at the southeast corner, he is regarded as the resident master. So, before any building work is begun, his permission is required, together with the approval of the gods holding him down. In return for seeking this permission, the Vastupurush protects the residents of the building.

Once the site of the mandir has been selected and ritually purified, the next stage in its erection is the laying out of the ground plan. Great importance is attached to the establishment of the mandir's ground plan because it functions as a sacred geometric diagram (*mandala*) representing the universe. The *mandala,* with its concentrically organized structure, is taken to be an image of the universe. By constructing this diagram to regulate the form of the mandir, a symbolic connection is created, binding together the world of the gods – the universe – and its miniature reconstruction through the work of man, the mandir. It is important to realize that *vastupurush mandala* for every site, state and country differs depending on various place-specific factors.

This visual representation of the Vastupurush as a governing device for making a building is called a *vastupurush mandala*. It is drawn as a square grid, but read as a concentric series of square shapes. The grid usually functions only as a means of zoning the different deities in the mandir.

The Vastupurush is visualized as lying inside the *mandala* with his face and stomach touching the ground and his arms and legs so folded as to cover the whole area as if he is carrying the weight of the structure. His head is pushed into the northeastern (*ishanya*) corner of the square and his legs are at the southwestern corner (*nairutya*), but he keeps changing his position throughout the year.

The body of the Vastupurush is regarded as being sensitive at a number of points called *marmas*, which lie at the intersection of major diagonals of the *vastupurush mandala* grid. It is important to avoid injury to the *marmas*, since the well-being of the Vastupurush assures the well-being of the building and, by implication, its owner. Thus, texts prohibit any direct construction upon the *marmas* themselves. So, no pillar, wall, door or window should be placed upon these points. This is achieved by shifting the centre line of the pillar, door, etc. by half the dimension of the point.

The *vastushastras* describe the use of a *vastupurush mandala*, 'divine chart', as a ritual ground plan in the construction of mandirs and other buildings. It is, in fact, not the actual plan of the mandir but a ritual diagram.

The earliest description of the *vastupurush mandala* is found in Varahamihira's *Bruhatsamhita*, compiled in the sixth century.

The square shape of the *mandala* is symbolic of earth, signifying

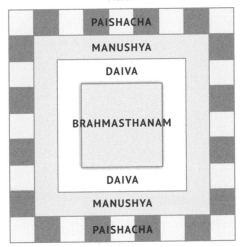

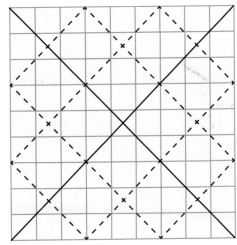

the four directions which bind and define it. The square is the archetype of order. Whereas, the circle represents a perfect shape, without beginning or end, signifying eternity and divinity.

The *vastupurush mandala* is the metaphysical design of mandirs and other structures. The square is divided into compartments and the diagonals are drawn. Each side of the square may comprise between 1 and 32 divisions, thus the number of smaller squares within the *vastupurush mandala* varies from 1 (1 by 1) to 1,024 (32 by 32). Each of these *mandalas* has specific names and is used in different settings, such as residential buildings, palaces, auditoriums, mandirs, etc.

The main *mandalas* are those with 1, 2, 3 and 7, 8, 9 divisions on each side. The most common are the 8 × 8 grid (= 64 squares) and the 9 × 9 grid (= 81 squares), widely used for mandirs and domestic dwellings.

The *vastupurush mandala* is divided into four concentric zones. The central area of each is called the *brahmasthanam*, and occupies a varying number of squares according to the size of the *mandala*: in *pitha* (9) and *upapitha* (25) it occupies one square, in *mahapitha* (16), *ugrapitha* (36) and *manduka* (64), four squares and in *sthandila* (49) and *paramasayika* (81), nine squares. The next three zones are *daiva*, *manushya* and *paishacha* areas and are said to denote enlightenment, consciousness and grossness respectively.

11

Principal Parts of a Mandir: Platform and Wall

PITHA, ADHISTHANA, JAGATI

The *Mayamatam* describes the pedestal or platform as that upon which a building rests. According to architectural treatises, a platform (called *pitha, adhisthana* or *jagati*) is used in mandirs to increase the final height of the main tower and to enhance structural stability. Also, the plinth provides a space to walk around the mandir structure.

VEDIBANDHA

Above the platform is the socle (called *vedibandha*) which serves as the wall base. The wall of the sanctum rises from the socle, which protrudes from under the bottom part of the wall. The socle should be strong as it carries the entire weight of the *garbhagruha*, the *mandap* and also the weight of the superstructures.

The socle has several distinctly named decorative mouldings, arranged from the bottom up in a specified order. The terminology varies according to the region and mandir style. In one *nagara* classification the mouldings are known as *bhit, kanpith, kumbho* and *kalsho*. It is not necessary that the base should have all these mouldings, however certain essential mouldings are seen in almost all mandirs. The mouldings spread the base beyond the vertical line so that the superstructure does not appear top heavy and gives greater stability and strength to the structure.

*Facing page:
Base and wall
of a mandir*

Shikhar

Chhaju

Keval 2
Keval 1
Bharani

Dodhiyo
Chhajli

Jangha

Machi

Keval

Kalasho

Kumbho

Kharo

Narathar

Ashvathar

Gajthar

Graspatti

Kanpith

Bhit (Pith)

Note: The colour of the mandir in this photograph has been digitally modified to highlight the different elements of a mandir

Such mouldings are also present to varying extents in other mandir structures, such as the *mahamandap, kalyan mandap* and *nrutya mandap.*

MANDOVAR

Above the *vedibandha* arises the the rear and side walls of the *garbhagruha*. The outer side of the *garbhagruha* walls, known as the *mandovar,* consists of a series of horizontal mouldings. From the bottom up these include: *kharo, kumbho, kalsho* and *keval (kapota)* In some mandirs, the mouldings are repeated several times. In between the mouldings there may be a carved recess called the *antarpatti,* which increases the vertical height of the wall and adds to the majesty of the mandir.

Vertically, projections and recesses of the wall result in niches and panels in which beautiful sculptures of gods, goddesses, sages and famous devotees are set. These vertical panels run from the *vedibandha* (base) to the *varandika* (entablature).

Demarcating the *mandovar* from the *shikhar* is the *varandika* (entablature or cornice), which itself usually has several mouldings. It extends out over the *mandovar* like a roof. Also known as *prastara,* the entablature serves as the base of the *shikhar*.

While the final Truth is to be encountered in the *garbhagruha,* or inner sanctum, the walls of the mandir provide manifestations of the Truth in many forms. This is to remind one that it is all a manifestation of the divine.

GAVAKSHA

An ornate window overhanging from a *shikhar* or exterior wall of the *garbhagruha* is known as the *gavaksha.*

The *gavaksha* may be round, triangular, rectangular or hexagonal. It has a jutting roof supported by elaborate pillars which hides a sealed, recessed window, often in the form of an intricately carved stone grill.

A question may arise: If the window is permanently closed, why construct it in the first place? Although the *gavaksha* endows the mandir with further majesty, its presence is more spiritual than ornamentation. Symbolically, the enshrined divinity sends forth his effulgence across the world through the *gavaksha*. Thus, although light may not enter, it is believed that it exits through the windows.

The *gavaksha* is a window for God enshrined within the *garbhagruha* to look out at the world. The *gavaksha* is found facing

Jharukho

Dodhiyo

Chhajli

Thambhli

Kakshasan

Jharukho

Asanpatt

Vedika

Rajsen

Daso

Keval

Kalasho

Kumbho

Kharo

Kanpith

Bhit

ADI Tour

different directions on the mandir walls, thus enabling God to grace
and make the entire world holy through his glance.

Gavaksha is a Sanskrit word and is a conjunction of 'gau', meaning
sun or sun rays, and 'aksh' meaning eye or axis of a heavenly body,
axle or discus. Scholars clarify the meaning of *gavaksha* as 'the eyes
of God in the form of the sun's rays' or 'a discus of sun rays'. Thus
the brilliant discus protects the mandir from evil influences.

God pulls the darkness of ignorance and material desires from
the devotee's soul and expels it through the *gavaksha*. In return he
gifts luminosity (knowledge) to the worshipper standing before
the *garbhagruha*.

Frequently, the *gavaksha* is decorated with a lion – a solar animal.
The lion is a power of God which leaps to protect the devotee from
misery and spiritual ignorance.

Gavaksha also means 'cow's eyes' and is also used to describe
the horseshoe-shaped design which is a feature of many mandirs.

JHARUKHO

A *jharukho* is a balcony juttting out from a wall. It may be at a
height above the ground or be connected to the ground by a series
of decorative layers. The *jharukho* may be sealed or accessible so
that people can enter and look out from the balcony.

Mandirs of multiple storeys provide greater scope for decorative
balconies.

SUSIDIARY SHRINES

Surrounding the main shrine, *garbhagruha*, are smaller shrines,
usually at the corners of the platform, which house *murtis* of other
deities or revered personalities. Vertically, these shrines consist of
a *vedibandha, mandovar, varandika* and small *shikhar*. Some may
even have a preceding *ardha mandap*.

12

Principal Parts of a Mandir: Garbhagruha, Mandaps and Ceilings

GARBHAGRUHA

The most auspicious element in the entire mandir complex is the *garbhagruha*, the sanctum sanctorum. It is here that the *murti* of the divine is enshrined. And it is for the worship of this enshrined *murti* that the devotee visits the mandir. The *garbhagruha* is an enclosed cella and its continuity is broken only by the entrance in the front wall, through which the devotee has darshan.

There is no inlet for natural light. If the door is closed, the interior is shrouded in complete darkness, except for the obligatory *divo*. Far from being the expected highly decorative majestic court, the *garbhagruha* is windowless, and its interior is simple and without intricate sculpted designs, in contrast to its exterior. It is as if it is decorated in inverse proportion to its spiritual importance.

The *garbhagruha* is known by a variety of names, depending on geographic location. In the north it is usually called *prasada* or *mula-prasada*, but in Orissa is known as *deul*. In the south, it is generally called the *vimana*, but in Tamil Nadu is known as the *kovil*. The word 'garbha-gruha' means 'womb-chamber' and represents the womb that gives rise to all creation.

Whatever the label, it houses the principle deity and its entire

*Facing page:
Garbhagruha (sanctum)
of the Vamana Mandir,
Khajuraho, Madhya Pradesh*

(Photo courtesy: Shay Bertling)

Left: Dwarshakh at
the entrance of a
sanctum sanctorum
Right: Pranala – spout
from which lustral water
exits the sanctum

structure is designed to resemble Mount Meru. It can be of various shapes: square, rectangle, octagon or circle; the *Bruhatsamhita* describes 20 shapes for a *garbhagruha*. The most common, however, is square.

In *nagara* mandirs, the basic shapes are modified by vertical projections on the outside walls. This gives rise to a variety of star-like shapes externally. Inside, however, the shape is unchanged. The vertical projections of the *nagara* superstructure and horizontal divisions of the *dravida* superstructure lead to the apex of the *shikhar*. Both of these symbolize the ascent from the square base, representing earth, of the *garbhagruha* to the circular finial, representing heaven, of the *shikhar*. This symbolizes man's spiritual quest from the mundane (square) to the divine (circle).

In addition to heightening the mystery of the divine presence, the shutting off of air and light to the *garbhagruha* also had a practical side – it helped to preserve the *murti*, which, in olden days, was often made of wood.

The *murti* in the *garbhagruha* is raised on a special platform – called a *sinhasan*, which may be of intricate design and gold-plated to emphasize its importance as the seat of God.

Threshold of
sanctum sanctorum,
BAPS Swaminarayan Mandir,
Ahmedabad, Gujarat

DWARSHAKH – DOOR FRAME

The *dwarshakh* (door frame) of the *garbhagruha* comprises
the two vertical jambs supporting the lintel containing a central
dedicatory block. The lower horizontal step is known as the
umbro (threshold, sill). It is positioned in the centre of the front
garbhagruha wall to a small height from ground level, linking the
two vertical jambs.

The jambs are carved as vertical sections or mouldings, some
projecting and others recessed. *Dwarpals* may be positioned at
the base of the jambs. The lintel may contain panels of gods and
goddesses or may be ornamented with various designs.

The threshold projects outwards with a semi-circular moulding
in the centre, on each side of which is a projecting *kirtimukh* face.
The floor space between the projecting threshold and the ground
floor of the *antarala* or *mandap*, as the case may be, may be filled
with an elaborately carved slab. The semicircular shape symbolizes
the transition from the worldly realm (traditionally represented
by a square) and the divine realm (represented by a circle). The
kirtimukh symbolizes that man must devour or overcome his base
nature to become pure and so be able to approach and reside with
God.

Pillared *mandap* of
Vijaya Vitthala Mandir,
Vijayanagara, Karnataka

MULTIPLE GARBHAGRUHAS

Early mandirs had only one *garbhagruha*, though some did have subsidiary shrines in which other deities were consecrated. Later, mandirs with multiple *garbhagruhas* were built. Today, many mandirs are built with multiple *garbhagruhas* connected under one roof, and housing multiple *murtis*. Also, over time, the *garbhagruha* has come to be furnished with modern artificial lighting to enable darshan of the consecrated deity throughout the day and other features that help to preserve the enshrined *murtis*.

The *garbhagruha* is a sanctuary from which outside influences are cut off by thick walls and narrow doors. The interior is kept secret and its sacredness is protected from mundane external influences. It is the place towards which the devotee proceeds to offer worship.

The sanctum enshrining the main deity may be encased by an outer wall. Between the inner and the outer walls, there is an intervening passage for circumambulation, called *sandhara*, running all around.

PRANALA

The *pranala* (water chute) also known as *gaumukh* or *ovu* is an

Ardha mandap or *roop choki* – portico leading into the *mahamandap*; Bruhadeshvar Mandir, Thanjavur, Tamil Nadu

important part of the *garbhagruha* and is for draining out lustral (*abhishek*) water from the sanctum.

It is of different shapes, e.g., circular, square, rectangular, faceted, etc. Apart from its ritualistic need it is an excellent architectural piece. The terminal end of the spout often looks like *vyala* (a mythical animal) or a *gaumukh* (the face of a cow).

MANDAPS

Initially, the sanctums existed in isolation. However, subsequently, to protect worshippers who gathered outside the sanctum from the rain and sun, thatched rectangular structures were erected. Also, as the role of the mandir in society expanded, more activities were conducted within the mandir premises and so facilities to enable these were built. Preserving the *garbhagruha* as the focal point, ancillary halls of varying sizes and ornamentation were built.

A *mandap* is any roofed, open or closed hall resting on pillars, standing independently or connected to the sanctum of the mandir.

Antarala or *korimandap* is a narrow intermediary space linking the *garbhagruha* and *mahamandap*. Initially, it was open from above, but later the space was enclosed. It may have niches in the side walls in which a deity is consecrated.

Sculpted stone ceiling in
Saumyakeshava Mandir,
Nagamangala, Karnataka

MAHAMANDAP

The main hall, called *mahamandap* or *navaranga*, is a pillared hall in front of the *garbhagruha*, built for worshippers to gather to honour the consecrated deity. It is also used for congregational services like festival rituals, singing and other collective acts of devotion. The *mahamandap* is usually of a larger size than the *garbhagruha* and is often decorated with pillars and sculptured designs. The ceilings are often decorated with motifs, sculptures and intricate floral, geometric and other designs. Above, the *mandap* is identified by either a *shikhar* or dome (*ghummat*), though its vertical height is less than the *garbhagruha shikhar*.

In some mandirs, there are *bhoga mandaps*, where offerings are made to the deities; *kalyan mandaps*, where the marriage ceremony of the principal deity and his consort is annually celebrated, and *nrutya mandaps*, where artistic performances are presented. In Shiva mandirs, preceding the *garbhagruha* there may be a Nandi Mandap with a statue of the sacred bull Nandi, looking at the statue or the *ling* of Shiva.

ARDHAMANDAP: FRONT PORTICO

The *ardhamandap* or *roop choki* is a pillared porch added at the front of the *mahamandap*. It is usually decorated with sculptures and symbolic designs. It serves as an extra stage for worshippers to pass through and reflect as they proceed from the disorderly mundane world towards the divine serenity of the deity in the main sanctum.

In mandir architecture, such transition zones are common and important. They symbolize the necessity to reflect, introspect and focus on one's spiritual quest.

While approaching the *garbhagruha* through the halls in front of it, the devotee is enclosed within the sacred architecture. Surrounding him are intricately designed pillars, domes and arches. Wherever his eyes may fall, he sees holy *murtis* and symbols. The atmosphere is soothing, as the scent of flowers, burning oil lamps and incense pervade the air. The devotee is being prepared for his encounter with God.

The mind becomes quiet, losing touch with the material world beyond the confines of the mandir. The senses – eyes, ears, nose, tongue and skin – experience only that which is related to God. The carvings cease at the door of the *garbhagruha*. Here they confront the devotee for the last time as he approaches the innermost sanctuary. He himself is not allowed to step inside the *garbhagruha*, since access to the *garbhagruha* is restricted to the mandir priests.

The dimness of the *garbhagruha*, illuminated only by an oil lamp or *divo* (modernity has replaced it with electric lights) is in stark contrast to the bright light outside in the open. The devotee is primed to concentrate all his energies on God.

The relaxing atmosphere created by the sacred architecture also encourages meditation, as the mind becomes silent.

CEILINGS

Inside the *mandaps*, the ceilings may form a dome or be flat. To form a dome, richly carved concentric courses are assembled on top of a framework provided by beams which rest on pillars. The number of concentric courses varies according to the height of the dome. At the apex of the dome, an exquisitely sculpted keystone is placed.

The ceilings are embellished with floral and geometric designs, sculptures, and scenes depicting scriptural stories and the lives of deities.

13

Principal Parts of a Mandir: Pillars and Arches

Pillars are derived from Vedic altars. To prepare temporary *mandaps* for public Vedic rituals, four pots filled with rice grains were placed at the corners of a square area. Banana tree stalks were placed within the pots and held upright by using rice grains as packing. These pots with stalks served as struts on which the cloth covering for the canopy was tied. Thus, the banana stalk can be regarded as an early pillar or column. Also, the rice-filled pots, with leaves and flowers emerging represent life – a recurring symbol in Hindu mandir architecture, known as *ghata-pallava*.

Pillars provide the structural support for the beams which rest on them to take the whole load of the *mandap* superstructure. Pillars are erected in the inner area of *mandaps* and in between walls. When attached to the walls they are known as *ardha-sthambhas* or pilasters. All visible surfaces of pillars are usually carved with intricate designs or embellished with statues.

Pillars comprise of three vertical sections: *kumbhi* (base), *sthambha* or *jangha* (shaft – the pillar proper) and *shirsha* (capital). Each section has mouldings which correspond to the wall mouldings.

The *kumbhi* (base) corresponds to the *kumbho* of the *mandovar*, and also may have other mouldings on top. Beneath it is the *khadsal*.

The *sthambha* (pillar shaft) may be a single piece or multiple stacked pieces.

The *shirsha* (capital) is the uppermost element and enlarges the

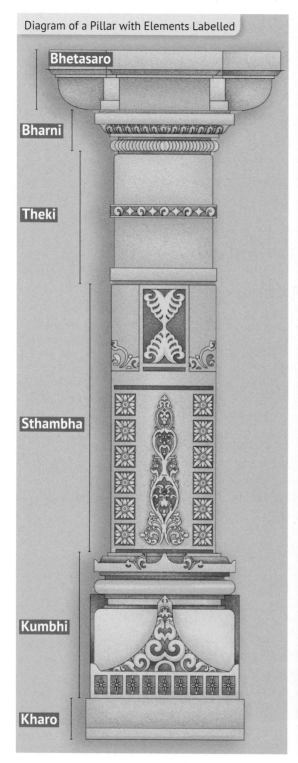

Diagram of a Pillar with Elements Labelled

Bhetasaro

Bharni

Theki

Sthambha

Kumbhi

Kharo

Hazari Ram Mandir, Hampi, Karnataka

Jalakanteshwar Mandir, Vellore, Tamil Nadu

Surya Mandir, Modhera, Gujarat

Ramanathaswamy Mandir, Rameshwaram, Tamil Nadu

Toran of Surya Mandir, Modhera, Gujarat

Kakshasan in Shamlaji Mandir, Shamlaji, Gujarat

pillar's support surface area with the structures above it. Beneath the capital is the *kanthasaru*, which has small extensions to serve as supports for statues or *torans*.

Pillars are described and classified on the basis of their cross-section shape: square, circle, polygon (faceted), scalloped (fluted), lobed, staggered, stellate. The cross-section may vary from base through to the capital and a single pillar may have a combination of shapes.

In cases where the pillar is in the *parikrama*, a *theki* is placed beneath the *kumbhi* to raise the column to the level of the *mandap* floor.

Pillars are placed at equal distances from each other to enable appropriate distribution of the superstructure load above them. Pillars may be embellished with mouldings featuring designs of flora, fauna geometric shapes and sculptures. Among the most common design is the vase and foliage (*ghata-pallava*) design.

TORAN – ARCH

A *toran* is an arch in between pillars which provides a decorative connection. It serves as a welcoming gate under which visitors pass and is a prominent feature of Gujarat mandirs.

It is used as both an architectural element and a ornamental feature. The arch may be flat, semi-circular, triangular, bow-shaped or of any other suitable shape. It emerges from the pillar either directly from the lower part of the capital or from the sculpted mouth of an elephant or *makara*.

Torans are often decorated with carvings of gods, sages, flowers, leaves, creepers, lions and other real or mythical animals.

Functionally, the *toran* provides a support from which to hang the *hindolo* (swing) in which the deity is placed on festive occasions.

KAKSHASAN – SEAT

A *kakshasan* is a seat with a sloping backrest that is attached to pillars or *mandap* walls. In the case of the latter, the wall height is limited by the height of the *kakshasan* backrest. The outer surface of the *kakshasan* has embellished with intricate carved designs, sculptures or scriptural scenes.

14

Principal Parts of a Mandir: Shikhar

SHIKHAR

The *shikhar*, marks the location of the *garbhagruha* and rises directly above it. This is an expression of the ancient ideal believing that gods reside in the mountains. Indeed, in South India the mandir spire is frequently carved with images of gods, with the *shikhar* being conceived as Mount Meru, the mystical mountain-axis of the universe.

The *shikhar* (meaning, mountain peak) is both the physical and spiritual axis of the mandir. Symbolizing the upward aspiration of the devotee, it is a potent metaphor for his ascent to enlightenment.

In North Indian mandir architecture, the *shikhar* is the superstructure, tower, pinnacle or spire above the sanctuary and also above the pillared *mandaps* (porches, pavilions or halls); it is the most eye-catching characteristic of the *nagara* style Hindu mandir. The *nagara* style *shikhar* is of five main types or modes, described below.

1. Latina

The *latina* spire is curvilinear in outline. It is the earliest type and from about the 5th century CE it is found above the sanctuary. The *latina shikhar* is composed of a series of horizontal roof slabs gradually receding toward the top and provided with vertical projections that extend from the base and wall of the mandir. The

*Facing page:
Nagara style shikhar of
a mandir in Mandore,
near Jodhpur, Rajasthan*

Left: Latina mode:
Galaganatha Mandir,
Pattadakal, Karnataka

Right: Shekhari mode:
Rajarani Mandir,
Bhuvaneshwar, Odisha

surface of the *shikhar* is covered with a vinelike tracery composed of diminutive *chandrashalas* (ogee arches). Above the truncated top (*skandha* – shoulder) rests a large grooved disk (*amalsar* or *amalak*), above which sits a pot as a crowning finial. The superstructure is marked into storeys (*bhumis*) by ribbed stones set into the corner bands of the *latina* tower. These details are inherited by the later modes.

The texture and dynamics of the *latina* depend largely on configurations of horseshoe arch (called *gavaksha*) patterns (their sinuous lines giving the central spine of the superstructure the name *lata*, meaning 'creeper,' hence *latina*). Examples of this type of superstructure are found at the Galaganath Mandir at Pattadakal and the Shatrughneshvar Mandir at Bhuvaneshvar.

2. Shekhari

The *shekhari* tower is a multi-spired variety of the *nagara shikhar* derived from the *latina* form in which multiple smaller half and quarter spires are attached to the main spire. It was first used in central and western India in the tenth century. The *shekhari* mode consists of the central *latina* spires with one or more rows of half spires added on either side and miniature *shikhars* clustered along the

base and corners. The Lakshman and Kandariya Mahadev mandirs at Khajuraho, Madhya Pradesh, are excellent examples.

Smaller secondary towers (*urushrungs*) on the mandir's exterior lead the eye up to the highest point. Their shape often replicates that of the tallest central tower, and serves to draw the eye upward towards it.

3. Bhumija

The *bhumija* type of superstructure gives a visual impression of multiple storeys of miniature spires rising up the main *shikhar* organized in horizontal bands. It was first used in the Malwa region, in western Madhya Pradesh, and then became popular in Gujarat and Rajasthan. The *bhumija* variation has a flat vertical projection in the centre of each of the four sides, the quadrants between being filled with rows of miniature shrines all the way up to the top of the tower. An example is the 11th-century Udayeshvar Mandir at Udayapur, Madhya Pradesh.

4. Vallabhi

The *vallabhi* spire is a barrel-vaulted superstructure resting on a raised *shikhar* and positioned at right angles to the entrance of a

Left: *Vallabhi* mode:
Teli-ka Mandir, Gwalior,
Madhya Pradesh

Right: *Phamsana* mode:
Surya (Sun) Mandir,
Gop, Gujarat

rectangulr *garbhagruha*. Examples include the Vaital Deul at Bhuvaneshwar, Orissa and Teli-ka Mandir at Gwalior, Madhya Pradesh. After the *latina*, it is the earliest alternative *nagara* mode, and the only one without the *latina shikhar* as an essential component.

5. Phamsana

The *phamsana shikhar* lacks any curvature as it rises and is found atop shrines and *mandaps* with a square ground plan. The *phamsana* is rectilinear in outline and capped by a bell-shaped member, a form more usually found above the *mandap*. Examples include the Surya Mandir at Gop in Gujarat and the Brahma Mandir at Khajuraho, Madhya Pradesh.

This style of *nagara shikhar* is regarded as the precursor to the *samvaran* superstructure used above some shrines.

DRAVIDA

Dravida superstructures are dominated by horizontal mouldings dividing the structure into separate storeys of decreasing size.

In South Indian architecture texts, the term *shikhar* is reserved for the dome-shaped crowning cap, though art historians have generally used the term to designate all mandir spires, north and

south. The South Indian spire, known as the *kutina* type, is different in shape from the North Indian *shikhar* and has a pyramidal storied arrangement, with each higher storey (*bhumi*) stepped and of diminishing size.

SHUKANASA

The *shukanasa* is the superstructure above the *antarala*, or intermediary passage between the *garbhagruha* and the *mahamandap*. *Shuka* means 'parrot' and *nasa* means 'nose'. It seems to be named as such due to its unususal shape. Its shape is derived from a curvilinear shikhar and so is present as a frontal projection predominently in mandirs with such a superstructure shape. The height of the *shukanasa* varies from about one-quarter to a half the height of the *shikhar*. As a general rule, its height is kept to the level of the superstructure above the *mandap*.

In some mandirs, the *antarala* is crowned with a *prasadputra*, which is a small *shikhar* (see p. 176 for example).

AMALAK

Amalak is a Sanskrit word for the fruit *Emblic Myrobalan* (Indian Gooseberry).

Dravida style *shikhar*: Airavateshvar Mandir, Darasuram, Tamil Nadu

Architectural Component

Amalak (also, *amalsar*) is the serrated crown or cogged disc that typically surmounts mandirs of the northern type. It is a ribbed, doughnut-shaped stone crowning the *nagara shikhar* and supports a pot finial known as a *kalash*. It is also used as the cushion-shaped portion of the capital in some columns.

Architecturally, *amalaks* function on *shikhars* as a terminal *amalak* on the central spire, as a crowning *amalak* on subsidiary spires and as corner *bhumi-amalaks* to mark the spire into storeys (*bhumis*).

Seed and Fruit

The construction of the mandir begins with the burying of seeds in a pot in the foundation. This seed is conceptually transposed through the crowning *amalak* upon completion of construction.

The *amalak* serves to remind the approaching worshipper that there is something beyond the fruit which must be strived for. The mandir is the place where one can obtain the elixir of life and immortality (*amrut*), for which the gods and demons churned the cosmic ocean. The *amalak* fruit is emblematic of this nectar.

Significance

In Indian religions, dharma is conceived of as a wheel. Just as the spokes of a wheel keep it in motion and in balance, dharma is that which holds the universe together and stops everything from flying apart. Therefore, the *amalak* is appropriately called a 'cogged wheel' and is an emblem for dharma. A mandir is a place to strive for union with the divine. The *amalak* has the role of reminding devotees that this striving consists of efforts and action in accordance with dharma. Since it holds the *kalash* in postition, the *amalak* symbolizes security and stability at the site of union between the mortal and immortal worlds.

KALASH

No mandir is complete without the *kalash*. The *amalak* crowns the *shikhar* and above the *amalak* is the *kalash*, the auspicious pot finial, which is the crowning glory of the superstructure. The *kalash* is symbolic of the immortalizing nectar-filled *kalash* that was churned out of the ocean with 13 other treasures by the gods and demons. Drinking even a drop of nectar would guarantee immortal life – victory over death. The *kalash* symbolizes blessings and wellbeing and man's eternal quest for immortality.

Shukanasa of dravida style Virupaksha Mandir, Pattadakal, Karnataka

The *kalash* is a systematic succession of various parts placed on top of each other. At the base is the *padgrahi*, then in turn the *andak, griva, padma pattika, karnika* and the *bijpur.*

Interestingly, the *kalash* placed on top of the superstructure is not embedded into the mandir structure by using mortar or cement. It is, in fact, held in position by a hollow rod that juts out of the *amalak* and runs through the *kalash.*

During the early period of mandir building the *kalash* was usually of stone. Later, *kalashes* made of copper were introduced, followed by those of brass. Some were gilted with gold. Just as the *kalash* placed in the depths of the foundation directly below the *garbhagruha* is worshipped and filled with nine sacraments, the *kalash* atop the *amalak* is likewise worshipped before being placed in position. The sacraments symbolize progress, expansion and wealth. When placed atop the *shikhar*, Vedic rituals are performed in which lay devotees enthusiastically participate.

An invisible stream of divine energy is created between the *kalash* in the foundations beneath the *garbhagruha*, the *murti* in the *garbhagruha* and the *kalash* atop the *amalak*. The centre of the energy stream is the *garbhagruha*. The *kalash* becomes a sacred antenna, capturing energy streams from the living spiritual world

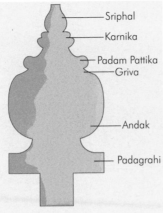

Sriphal
Karnika
Padam Pattika
Griva

Andak

Padagrahi

Left: Shikhar with an amalak and stone kalash, Mukteshwar Mandir, Bhuvaneshwar, Orissa

Middle: Diagram of the various parts of a kalash

Right: Shikhar crowned with a golden amalak, kalash and a flag, Ambaji Mandir, Ambaji, Gujarat

which are channelled down through the *shikhar* where they are caught in the *garbhagruha* – the fountainhead of all energy.

DHAJA – FLAG

The *dhaja* or *dhvaja* represents the victory of good over evil. Just as kings exhibit their lordship over their kingdom by hoisting a special flag that carries the royal emblem, the *dhaja* over a mandir signifies the sovereignty of God, who is the supreme power, not just on earth but in the entire universe; which is, after all, his creation.

Mandirs in northern India have their *dhaja* on top of the *shikhar*. Southern Indian mandirs usually have a special flagpole (*dhvajasthambha*) raised in the courtyard in front of the mandir.

The devotee visits the mandir to gain victory over his base instincts of passion, anger, greed, jealousy, etc. Where there is God, there is victory. The mandir visit invigorates the devotee, recharging him with strength and bravery to face the hardships of daily life, knowing that ultimately those who have surrendered to the will of God find victory.

The *dhaja* and the flagpole encourage man to fly higher into the spiritual sky releasing himself from the bonds of material life to soar into God-realization.

15

Principal Parts of a Mandir:
Gopuram and Compound

SOPANA

The approach to the sanctum is through the *sopana* – the stairs. They are usually built at the front from the ground level to the level of the *ardhamandap*. There are two types of *sopana:* (i) direct flight of stairs with balustrades on either side or (ii) lateral flights of steps meeting at a common platform at the top of the steps. These steps have banisters on either side. The sides of direct steps and the front of lateral steps may have carvings of various designs. There may also be stairs leading to the *mahamandap* at the sides – again direct or meeting at a platform.

DHVAJASTAMBHA – FLAGPOLE

The *dhvajasthambha* (flagpole) in front of either the *garbhagruha* or *antarala* or the *mandap* is another common feature, especially of South Indian mandirs.

The old texts favoured wooden or bamboo poles, and the flagpole was not a permanent structure. The ceremony of flying the mandir flag marked the inauguration of a major festival. The old customs required that no major domestic auspicious functions be held in the village while the mandir flag is hoisted. This was perhaps to suggest that the celebrations at the mandir took precedence and everyone in the village should participate in them.

Over time the permanently fixed flagpole became a common

Facing page:
Gopuram of
Kapaleeshvar Mandir,
Mylapore, Chennai,
Tamil Nadu

feature in mandir architecture. The older mandirs had flagpoles made of stone. This led to a stone pillar or wooden pole covered with copper, brass or even gold-plated and installed on a raised stone platform in front of the sanctum. The top portion of this tall mast will have three horizontal perches (symbolizing righteousness, reputation and prosperity, or the three divinities, Brahma the Creator, Vishnu the Preserver and Shiva the destroyer), pointing towards the sanctum.

Dipasthambha

BALIPITHA

The *balipitha* is a lotus-shaped stone or the footprints of the deity on a pedestal. It is where offerings in the form of water, flowers, sesame seeds, rice, etc. are placed daily at specific times to the accompaniment of traditional musical instruments and chanting of hymns. It is usually made of hard granite and is ornate and majestic.

DIPASTHAMBHA

The *dipasthambha* (lamp post) holds *divos* (small flame lamps) and is often situated in front of the *balipitha*. It varies in design, for example, a bud-shaped chamber may be at top or there may be holders placed at intervals along the length of the post to receive the lamps. It illuminates the mandir court during night time through the light of numerous lamps around the pillar.

WATER TANK

Some mandirs have a rectangular or apsidal water tank with steps leading to the water.

GOPURAMS AND PRAKARAS

In the case of major mandirs, the entire mandir area is surrounded by a series of concentric protective walls, the *prakaras*. Punctuating these walls are *gopurams*, the lofty entrance gateways. These rectangular, pyramidal towers, often fifty metres high dominate the skyline and have become the hallmark of southern mandir architecture. They are adorned with intricate and brightly painted sculptures of gods, humans, animals and other figures. The *gopuram* emphasizes the importance of the mandir within the city.

The practice of erecting a *gopuram* at the entrance gateway to the mandir seems to have begun during the mid-12th century. With

Water tank,
Meenakshi Mandir,
Madurai, Tamil Nadu

the decline of the mighty Cholas and with the increasing threat from invading armies, the mandir cities (prominently Madurai and Srirangam) found it necessary to erect a series of protective walls to safeguard and defend their mandirs, palaces and cities. The *gopurams* lead from one enclosure to the next and, initially, served as watch and defensive towers.

What started as a defensive structure rapidly developed into a prominent architectural feature with great visual appeal. The *gopurams* grew in size until the colossal ones rose to dominate the mandir complex, surpassing the main sanctum in height and grandeur. Some of them are extremely large and elaborately decorated with sculptures.

Among the finest examples are the Sundara Pandya Gopura (13th century) of the Jambukeshvar Mandir at Tiruchchirappalli and the *gopurams* of the great Shiva Mandir at Chidambaram.

The *gopurams* of the Meenakshi Mandir at Madurai (see p. 38) are also a magnificent array of towers. There are twelve impressive *gopurams* soaring over the three-tier *prakara* walls. The outer four towers dominating the city landscape are truly huge in size and magnificence.

The *gopurams* appear to have influenced revision in the

Dhvajasthambha, Bhootpuri

Left: Series of boundary walls (*prakaras*) with gopurams of varying size, Arunachaleshvar Mandir, Tiruvannamalai, Tamil Nadu

Right: Gopuram, Meenakshi Temple, Madurai, Tamil Nadu

mandir design and layout. The spaces around the shrine became hierarchical; the further the space was from the main shrine, the less its eminence.

Though the evolution of the *dravidian* mandir architecture stalled briefly after the demise of the Pandyan Empire, the architectural expression scaled new heights during the reign of the Vijayanagara kings (15th and 16th centuries). Although the later mandirs were not huge in size, they often were of very fine workmanship. For instance, the Subrahmanya Mandir of the 17th century, built in the Bruhadeshvar Mandir complex at Thanjavur, indicates the vitality of architectural traditions even at that late date.

Gopuram Structure

A *gopuram* is generally constructed with a massive stone base and a superstructure of brick and pilaster. It is rectangular in plan and topped by a barrel-vault roof crowned with a row of finials. It differs from the *vimana* in that it need not necessarily be square-based. Above that rectangular base a pyramidal structure covered

with a brightly coloured plethora of sculpture is raised to a great height. A typical *gopuram* is a building rising up into a tapering tower, often over forty-five metres in height, and entered by a rectangular doorway in the centre of its long side.

In the past, cities all over South India could be discerned from afar by the distinctive shape of their *gopurams* dominating the skyline. The name is derived from the 'cow-gate' of the Vedic village.

Symbolically, the *gopuram* and the entrance to the mandir represent the feet of the deity. A devotees bows at the entrance, the feet of the Lord, as he steps into the mandir and proceeds towards the sanctum, leaving behind the temporal world of contradictions and confusion.

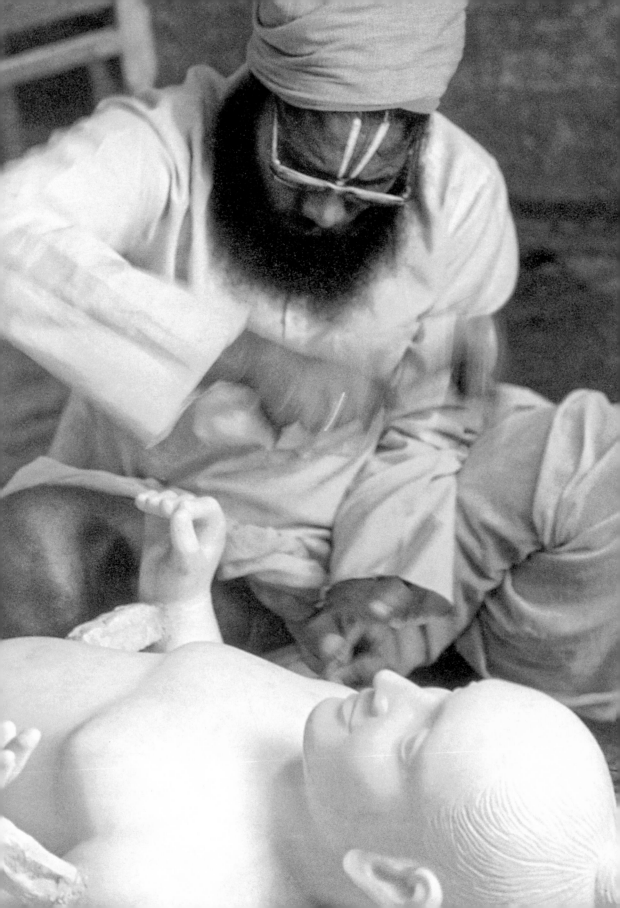

16

Murti Worship and Mandir Sculpture

MURTI WORSHIP

The underlying purpose for building mandirs is to enshrine the *murti* of God in the *garbhagruha*. In English *murti* is usually translated as 'icon' or 'image'.

The word icon is derived from the Greek *eikon* and is defined in the *Oxford Dictionary of English* as 'a person or thing regarded as a representative symbol or as worthy of veneration'. Thus, iconography is the study and interpretation of these 'visual images, symbols, or modes of representation'.

People of all faiths have always tried to visualize the Ultimate Reality by using words such as God, Lord, King, Emperor, etc. to generate mind pictures. Hindus, in addition to using word pictures, introduced the use of physical images. This nourishes the soul's spiritual quest by also engaging the sense of sight, instead of just remaining limited to words. In fact, images are particularly useful to those who cannot read and complements the spiritual experience of those who can.

Hindus firmly believe that God pervades everywhere and everything. For many millennia, Hindus have used symbols, natural and man-made, to help in their quest to experience the divine. The symbols used to represent divine beings are referred to as *murtis*. Made in a variety of materials of varying durability – clay, terracotta, wood, stone, metal and others – *murtis* are, in fact, part of a larger

*Facing page:
Artisan sculpting a
murti at a workshop
in Jaipur, Rajasthan*

Theriomorphic *murtis*:
icons with nonhuman features

Left: Shri Hanumanji

Right: Shri Nrusinhji

body of Indian sculpture which has developed within a highly complex, yet systematic, framework of methods and meanings. The earliest *murtis* discovered date back to the second millennium BCE and were found at Mohenjo Daro in the Indus Valley in present-day Pakistan.

In Vedic times, rituals played a central role in Hindu worship, so there was little need for *murtis*. However, as the bhakti tradition gradually replaced the more ritualistic tradition of the early Vedic era and a devotion predominant tradition developed, the use of *murtis* for worship increased. This enabled devotees to actively participate in worship rituals and offer bhakti. Previously, it had been the priests who performed worship rituals on behalf of the public.

As people attempted to connect with the divine, their visualizations resulted in a variety of artistic representations. The resulting *murtis* were an attempt to give a tangible form to abstract metaphysical concepts, and using these physical representations to connect with the unseen divine. In this way, devotees offered worship to a personal God as the *murtis* aided contemplation on the divine.

MURTI FORMS

Hindus revere 'iconic', or anthropomorphic (human-like), and 'aniconic', or nonanthropomorphic, *murtis*.

Aniconic *murtis:*

Top (L to R): Shivaling, Shaligram, Swastika

Bottom (L to R): Aum, Tulasi, Yantra

Iconic Murti

Some feel that portraying God in a human form reduces God to the human domain and diminishes his aura of divinity. However, such a possibility is prevented by adding distinctively supernatural features to the natural human features. For example, adding extra arms or heads, and using unnatural colours emphasize the divinity of the *murtis*. Also, combining human features with nonhuman features – such as, Nrusinhji with a lion head and torso, Ganeshji with an elephant head and Hanumanji with a monkey form – further serve to reduce the likelihood of misappropriating humanness to the *murti*. Such *murtis* with nonhuman attributes are called theriomorphic. Although not all *murtis* are fashioned with these fantastic forms – indeed, many are outwardly of normal human appearance – the understanding that the *murti* represents divinity is embedded in the Hindu psyche.

Aniconic Murti

Aniconic *murtis*, although they refer to a deity and are no less powerful, they do not resemble the anthropomorphic form. Examples of Hindu aniconic images include the *ling* of Shiva or the natural stone *shaligram* of Vishnu, the swastika, the written form of aum, the tulasi plant and the *yantra*.

In Vedic times, the fire altar represented the *murti* of the primordial creator, Prajapati. Even today, fire is used as an aniconic *murti* of the divine and has a central place in many Hindu rituals.

In the skilled hands of devoted artists, *murtis*, iconic or aniconic, depict the glory and sanctity of the deities. Thus, *murtis* consecrated in mandirs are usually man-made, but are endowed with divinity by virtue of their ritual consecration in accordance with the shastras. The divine manifests through the *murti* to awaken bliss and peace within the devotee. By meditating upon such a form, devotees awaken the best within themselves and are able to rise above the turmoil resulting from their own desires and base natures.

THE VARIETY OF MURTIS

The *murtis* used for worship are of three types:

1. *Sthavar (Achal)* – *murtis* which are consecrated permanently in the sanctum and are immovable. They are often large in size and heavy.

2. *Jangam (Chal)* – *murtis* which are portable and may be taken out of the sanctum for festival and ceremonial occasions. *Chala murtis* are generally small and/or lightweight to enable easy portability.

3. *Kshanik* – temporary *murtis,* usually made of clay, are for worship during a festival. At the end of the festival worship the *murti* is ritually submerged in a pond, river or sea.

The Shrimad Bhagwat (11.27.12) describes the use of eight different materials from which *murtis* for worship may be made:

शैली दारुमयी लौही लेप्या लेख्या च सैकती।
मनोमयी मणिमयी प्रतिमाऽष्टविधा स्मृता॥

Shaili dārumayi lauhi lepyā lekhyā cha saikati;
Manomayi manimayi pratimā'shtavidhā smrutā.

1. *Shaili*	Marble or other stone. The *murti* should be made from a single block of stone.
2. *Lauhi*	Metallic *murti,* made from pure metal or *panchdhatu* – commonly, a mixture of gold, silver, iron, copper, zinc. Sometimes, tin or lead are used as one of the metals.
3. *Darumayi*	Wooden.
4. *Lepya*	Made of sandalwood paste, clay or any other material which can be moulded.
5. *Saikati*	Sand. Used mainly for festivals.
6. *Lekhya*	Drawn, painted or etched.
7. *Manimayi*	Jewels or other crystals.

8. *Manomayi*　Imagined in the mind, not having a physical form as the above seven varieties.

SHILPASHASTRAS

Guidance for sculpting *murtis* is found in the *shilpashastras*, and the worship rituals to be offered by devotees to the *murti* are described in the Agamas. Canonical texts that detail the processes and rules governing iconography and iconometry include: *Bruhatsamhita* of Varahamihira (6th century CE), *Shukranithisara, Abhilashitartha Chintamini* by Someshwara (a 10th century western Chalukya king), *Caturvarga Chintamini* by Hemadri (13th century CE), *Kashyapa Shilpa Samhitha, Mayamata, Manasara, Shilparatna, Manollas, Kumaratantra, Lakshana Samuchayya, Rupamanada, Tantrasara* of Ananda Tirtha (Sri Madhvacharya) and *Vishnudharmottara Puran*.

CREATING A MURTI

Creating a *murti* is a special art. When making *murtis* of any type, craftsmen were expected to undertake ritual purification and meditate to visualize the final form of the *murti*, since their role was to attempt to depict the true nature of the reality that already exists. Apprentices learnt by memorizing and repeatedly practicing the techniques taught by their mentors. The novices were expected to

Metallic sculptures cast using the lost wax technique

learn and apply various calculations to ensure aesthetic proportions of the *murti*, but at the same time, they also had artistic freedom to enhance its beauty and appeal.

In ancient India, clay *murtis* had gained immense popularity, especially in north India due to the easy availability of clay and mud deposited by the north's many rivers. In addition, clay is easily worked upon by even the less talented *murti* makers.

Murtis of stone and metal are regarded as the best because of their lasting quality and since they are not easily damaged. The *Manasara* and *Manollas* treatises give detailed instructions about how to make a metallic *murti*.

Metal icons are generally made up of an alloy of five metals (*panchdhatu*): commonly, copper, zinc, iron, silver and gold. The process is known as *madhuchchhishtha vidya* – since the wax used in the processes was taken from beehives. These *murtis* were made using the lost-wax process, described in the *Manasara*: a detailed model is first meticulously prepared of hard beeswax, which is then covered with layers of clay. The clay-covered model is then heated so that all the wax melts and drains out. The cavity that remains is a clay mould of the original wax image. The molten metal alloy is poured into the toughened mould through channels made in the original design. Then the cast is buried in the earth for cooling. When it is completely cooled the outer clay shells are carefully broken and the stems of the channel are filed off. After annealing,

Murti of Lord Vishnu in *shayana* (reclining) posture

in which the image is heated in a furnace, the *murti* is cooled by immersion in water. As the wax model is lost each time, each bronze is a unique work of art.

The oldest such *murti* to have been found as yet in archaeological diggings has been dated to between 2500 to 1500 BCE.

MURTI ANATOMY

The *shilpashastra* texts deal with iconography and iconometry. For each particular deity, these works specify the correct proportions of the parts of the body, the appropriate postures, the required number of arms, the gestures of the hands (*mudra*), the emblems and weapons to be held in the hands (*ayudha*), and the appropriate mount (*vahan*).

The location of the shrine, climate and uses are all taken into consideration when deciding the material. The *murti* should thus be made perfect in every way as countless devotees will, through devotion to God manifest in the *murti,* be inspired to tread the spiritual path.

The arts of *shilpa* (sculpture) and *chitra* (painting) have their foundations in the *natyashastras* – the texts of the dancing arts. The postures (*asanas*), gestures (*mudras*) and flexions or curves (*bhangas*) of the sculpted *murti* are often static portrayals of dance poses.

POSTURES

The *shilpashastras* describe three basic postures of a *murti*: *sthanaka* (standing), *asana* (seated) and *shayana* (reclining).

Murtis in the *sthanaka* posture are the most common found in mandirs.

Shayana is the image of the deity in a reclining or sleeping position. In Hindu mandirs, only images of Vishnu are represented in this position.

Asana is when the deity is in a sitting posture.

MUDRA

Mudra is a gesture of the hands and fingers. There are in general two types of *mudras*, those with one hand and those with two hands. There are dozens of possible hand gestures based on dancing poses. The following are among the more important:

Abhay mudra: hand raised to shoulder level with palm facing the viewer. This gesture symbolizes that the devotee should remain fearless since the deity will protect.

Varada mudra: hand flexed at elbow and palm hanging downwards facing the viewer. It symbolizes that the deity is granting a boon to the devotee.

Jnan mudra: The thumb and index finger of the right hand join to form a circle, with the palm facing inwards. It conveys the message that knowledge (*jnan*) comes from within.

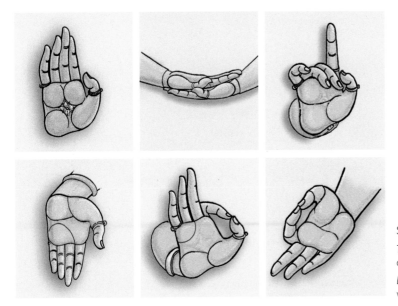

Some common *mudras*:

Top (L to R):
abhay, dhyan, suchi

Bottom (L to R):
varada, jnan, vyakhyan

Vyakhyan mudra: the thumb and index finger of the right hand meet and the palm faces the viewer. It symbolizes that knowledge is shared with others.

AYUDHA – EMBLEMS

In general use, the word *ayudha* refers to weapons; but, in iconography, it refers to whatever objects are held in the deity's hands. The *ayudhas* indicate the nature, character and functions associated with the deity. For instance, Saraswati holds in her hands a book symbolizing the Vedas and learning; a rosary symbolizing the cyclical nature of time; and a *veena,* a musical instrument symbolizing music and her benevolent nature. These objects are not weapons in the conventional sense, but the sculpturer employs them as symbols to expand, depict and interpret the nature of the deity.

Each of these *ayudhas* signifies a certain aspect of the deity or it stands for a concept. For instance, a mirror signifies a clear mind and awareness; a flag signifies victory or celebration; an *ankush* (goad) signifies exercising control over the senses and base instincts; *damaru* (small drum) in the hands of Shiva signifies creation and the origin of sound and learning; and, the sceptre signifies authority and rule of law. Apart from weapons a variety of objects are employed as *ayudhas.* These include instruments of various professions (pen, chisel, hammer, plow, sickle, etc.), musical instruments (flute, *veena,* drums, pipes, trumpets, etc.), plants and trees (*ashvattha, bilva,*

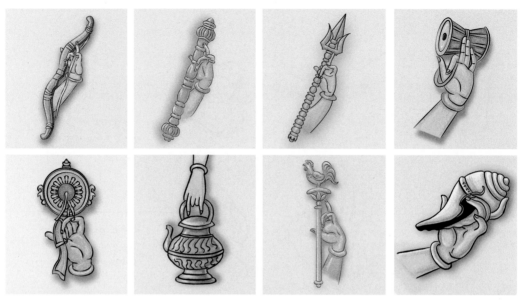

Ayudhas:

Top (L to R):
dhanushya (bow), *gada*
(goad), *trishul* (trident),
damaru (small drum)

Bottom (L to R):
chakra (discus), *kamandal*
(water pot), *rajdand* (sceptre),
shankh (conch shell)

paddy seeds, grass, etc.) and miscellaneous objects (mirror, bell, book, flag, lamp, vase, umbrella, etc.).

FLEXIONS

Regardless of the gestures of the hands and postures of the legs, the flexion of the *murti's* body is described relative to a central line that passes down the centre from the head through the forehead, nose, chin, chest, navel, genitals, and between the thighs and the feet.

The main types of *bhangas* are as follows:

Samabhanga: Whether standing or sitting, the whole body remains straight, unflexed and equally distributed along a central line. There is no sway in the body posture.

Abhanga: The body is slightly deflected from the centre at the head or waist with the weight more on one foot.

Tribhanga: The triple bend with body gracefully flexed at the neck, shoulders and waist.

Atibhanga: Known as the great bend, the body has several bends such that head, torso and limbs are in differing directions.

ALANKAR: ORNAMENTATION

The *shilpis* took great delight in adorning the *murti* with rich and finely carved ornaments. The *alankar* element offers the artists abundant scope to exercise their imagination and display their

| Samabhanga | Samabhanga | Abhanga | Tribhanga | Atibhanga |

Types of flexions or *bhangas*

ingenuity. Deities, male and female, are adorned with ornaments, or *alankars*, appropriate to their status. Often, the sculpted ornaments serve as the garments of an image.

Specific names are given to the ornaments that adorn various body parts of a *murti* (see illustration on p.116).

With regard to garments, the preference is to sculpt the bare body and not sculpt garments onto the *murti*. However, when used the body is recognizable by the patterns engraved on the shapes of the limbs. Bare *murtis* are adorned using specially fitted cloth garments and jewellery as ornamentation.

The *murtis* of the different deities are identified by their garments, ornamentation and coiffure (headdress), the emblems (*ayudhas*) in their hands, the mount (*vahan*) on which they are seated and other characteristic features. For example, Ram holds a bow, Shiva holds a trident (*trishul*), Vishnu holds a conch shell and discus (*chakra*), Durga is seated on a lion and Brahma has four faces.

MEASUREMENT SYSTEMS

The sacred *murtis* of the mandir are subject to strict mathematical criteria in the discipline of iconometry, the geometry of *murti*-making. Only a well-made *murti*, satisfactory in its proportional measurements, will be able to invite the deity to reside within it. Two systems of iconometry seem to have existed.

The first is a proportional system based on the *tala* unit of

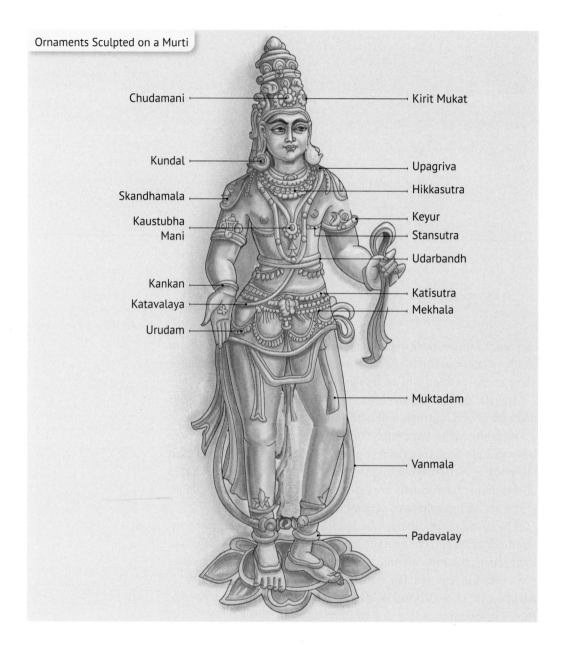

Chudamani

Kirit Mukat

Kundal

Upagriva

Skandhamala

Hikkasutra

Kaustubha
Mani

Keyur

Stansutra

Udarbandh

Kankan

Katisutra

Katavalaya

Mekhala

Urudam

Muktadam

Vanmala

Padavalay

measurement. One *tala* is equal to the length of the human face from the top of the forehead to the base of the chin. This facial length (called *mukham*) is measured in two ways: *kai tala* – equivalent to the length of the extended hand from the tip of the middle finger to the wrist of that person; and *kai chan* – equal to the distance between the middle finger and the thumb of the extended hand (see illustrations). One *tala* comprises of 12 *angulas*. One *angula* is

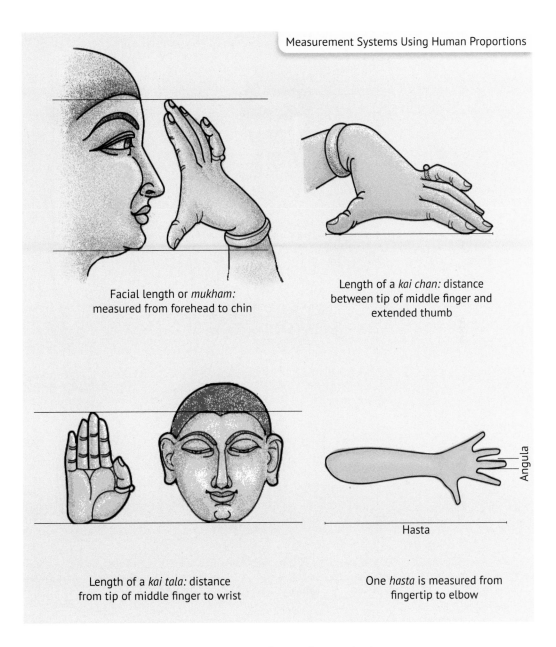

Facial length or *mukham:* measured from forehead to chin

Length of a *kai chan:* distance between tip of middle finger and extended thumb

Length of a *kai tala:* distance from tip of middle finger to wrist

Hasta

Angula

One *hasta* is measured from fingertip to elbow

the width of the middle finger between the first and second joints. In turn, one *angula* is comprised of 8 *yavai*. A *yavai* is the length of a barley rice grain. This system of proportional measurement is known as the *talamana* system. This system ensures the aesthetic symmetry and grace of the *murtis* and their spiritual significance.

The relative sizes of the various body parts are expressed in terms of the *tala*. For example, a *navatala* (9 *talas*) *murti* has the

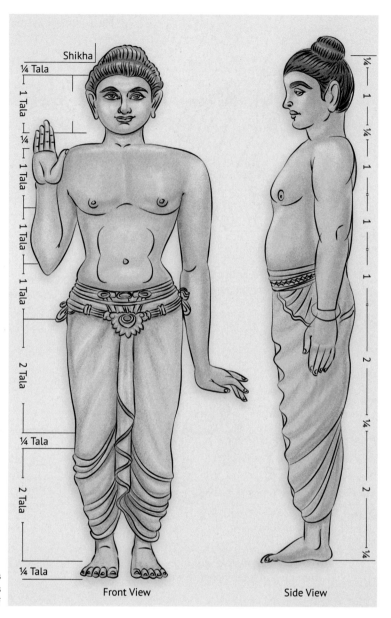

Front View

Side View

Front and side views
showing body proportions
of a 9 *tala murti*

following form: head – ¼ *tala*; face – 1 *tala*; neck – ¼ *tala*; chest – 1 *tala*; navel – 1 *tala*; genital belt – 1 *tala*; thigh – 2 *talas*; knee – ¼ *tala*; leg – 2 *talas*; foot – ¼ *tala*.

To describe the eyes, ears, nose, fingers and other smaller body parts, the *angula* and *yavai* are used.

Using this system, the shastras describe specific *tala* sizes for particular categories of *murtis*. The most important ones are

Dwarpals at the entrance of a shrine

navatala, *ashtatala* (8 *talas*), *saptatala* (7 *talas*) and *panchatala* (5 *talas*).

Since the Hindu mandir is depicted as representing the cosmic man (*purush*), it follows then that the system of measurement is related to the body. This system was predominantly used in South India, where *murtis* were commonly made using the *angula* measurement of the patron, reinforcing the belief that spiritual merit is acquired by such benevolence.

The second is a system of derived proportions. The stone or the block of wood selected for carving is divided into a number of equal parts. If the selected piece is divided into ten equal parts, the division is known as *dasatala*; if divided into nine equal parts then the division is known as *navatala* and so on. The *shilpashastras* generally prescribe a scale ranging from one (*ekatala*) to ten (*dasatala*), with each *tala* subdivided into 12 *angulas*. So, if the height of the *murti* is nine *tala*, the selected stone or wood is divided into 108 equal *angulas* before sculpting. This system was more common in North India; the material is divided into the required number of equal parts and the *murti* proportions derived accordingly.

DWARPALS: GUARDIANS

Dwarpals are the formidable looking 'gatekeepers' or guards in the service of the presiding deity of the mandir. They are the servants and

Narrative sculptures depict scriptural stories: The story of Abhimanyu trapped in the *chakravyuha* army formation during the Mahabharat War presented on the Hoysaleshvar Mandir, Halebid, Karnataka

protectors of their masters. They are typically depicted as huge and robust warriors. *Dwarpals* are placed in pairs, usually at the entrance to the mandir and also at the doorway to the sanctum (*garbhagruha*). General features of all *dwarpals* include: they are well built, tall, muscular, broad shouldered and are soldier-like. They carry weapons and are depicted as standing guards. *Dwarpals* placed on the exterior of entrances to guard the mandir from evil influences are usually more ferocious looking than those at the doorway to the sanctum.

SCULPTURES

The walls, pillars, bases, cornices and other mandir components are profusely embellished with sculptures of flora, fauna, humans, mythical forms, devas and other designs which enhance the beauty of the mandir. These sculptures may be carved out of the stone that comprises that structure or may be carved separately and then attached to the structure. These sculptures are produced in conformity with the *shilpashastras* and reflect the outstanding skill and creativity of the artisans.

Mandirs depict essential concepts through the use of 'narrative' and 'iconic' sculptures. Narrative sculptures show characters in

action, interacting with each other, and they often depict scenes from scriptural stories. Iconic sculptures show stationary characters exemplifying qualities for the observer to aspire towards. Narrative scenes attempt to educate, while iconic sculptures serve as a focus for devotion. Thus, sculptures are an integral part of mandirs.

EROTIC CARVINGS

To casual observers erotic (*mithun*) sculptures seem out of place: Why such things in a place of worship? However, within Hinduism spiritual ideas are demonstrated in many ways, of which *mithun* carvings are just one. They are, in fact, interpreted as symbolic portrayals of the state of 'union' with God. Despite this, such imagery accounts for only a tiny fraction of the iconography on most mandirs. Thus, it is not the iconographic priority of mandirs.

Mithun means 'the state of being a couple'. The Bruhadaranyak Upanishad says, "Just as a man closely embraced by a beloved woman knows nothing more without or within, so also a spiritual person embraced by God knows nothing more of what is without or within. This is his true form in which his (worldly) desire is satisfied. He has no desire or any pain" (IV 3.21). Thus, *mithun* is a human symbol of the total involvement in God required for *moksha*

Kirtimukh designs decorate mandir walls and arches

– ultimate release – from the material world and the life-death cycle. Such carvings are a reminder of the true goal in life – *moksha* – the attainment of pure divine bliss by being totally engrossed in God.

Many theories have attempted to understand this component of mandir architecture, resulting in perpetuation of misinterpreted ideas relating to this theme. Devangana Desai, in an extensive study on the temples of Khajuraho, has furnished the discussion with a more nuanced understanding of perhaps why these sculptures are present on some structures:

1. *Mithun* figures are in fact not reflective of the *Kama Sutra* text, since such a secular treatise has historically never determined the iconographic programme of a mandir. The tradition of *mithun* imagery (as seen on Hindu, Jain and Buddhist monuments) in fact predates the *Kama Sutra*.

2. While some imagery no doubt is reflective of the spiritual aspiration of non-duality, or oneness with a higher power, other images serve as satricial commentary on lewd practices that are meant to be overcome.

3. Such images serve as magico-defensive auspicious motifs in order to avert evil, death and misfortune.

4. *Mithun* imagery in mandir sculpture is justified since they

illustrate *kama,* which is one of the four *purusharths* (endeavours) of human life leading to *moksha.* Hence, the *mithuns* are not to be seen as vulgar sculptures. Further in terms of yoga philosophy, *mithun* imagery could symbolically represent the joining of two essences, the mundane and trans-mundane, the earthly and the divine.

5. They are present to serve as a *yantra* device on the architecture itself. A study of some mandirs, such as those at Khajuraho, shows that erotic imagery was strategically placed on the juncture points of the temples. The underlying geometry of these images can be associated with auspicious protective diagrams or *yantras,* and as such the placement of these images on juncture areas symbolically reinforced those points that were considered vunerable or weak in the structure of the mandir.

KIRTIMUKH

The *kirtimukh,* face of glory, is a lion-like sculpture with horns, lolling tongue and huge bulging eyes. The lion is a symbol of justice and power. The face of glory is also known as *grasmukh* – the devourer – and *rahumukh* – the eclipser. It is also known as Kal – Time, the destroyer of all. The three horns unite the three natures of the Lion, Dragon and Time, and also signify the coming together of the past, present, and future in the divine power that controls all.

The *kirtimukh* is sometimes an incomplete face with no lower jaw, symbolizing the Hindu belief that the soul is reborn until it attains ultimate liberation.

It also symbolizes the monstrous nature of one's existence due to the wicked effects of one's inherent base nature. It serves as a reminder that such evil nature must be overcome to truely enjoy the bliss of God.

The *kirtimukh* is thus a surprisingly complex combination of symbols.

17

Mandir Rites

In the Hindu tradition, rituals are performed at all important stages during the construction of a mandir, from the moment of selecting a suitable building site, right up to the completion of the entire project when the *murtis* are consecrated, and even afterwards. Among the more important rituals performed are: *bhumipujan, shilanyas vidhi,* consecration of first pillar, *pujan* of *garbhagruha dwarshakh, amalsar pujan* and *murti-pratishtha* (including *yagna,* and *pujan* of *kalashes* and *dhvajasthambhas*). Thereafter, the *patotsav* ceremony is performed annually to commemorate the anniversary of the *murti-pratishtha.*

BHUMIPUJAN

Once the site is selected and its suitability for construction is confirmed, the first ceremony performed is that of *bhumipujan.*

The *bhumipujan* ceremony involves paying homage to the land and comprises prayers asking the land for permission to disturb its natural state for construction work. Such is the reverence Hinduism holds for nature.

SHILANYAS

The foundation stone-laying ceremony, called the *shilanyas vidhi,* is the laying of the first stone or brick to signify the start of construction. The foundations are first dug and in the area directly below where the *garbhagruha* will be built and the *murti* enthroned, a deeper pit is dug.

The ceremony is specifically designed to purify the land by

removing any evil influences that may be permeating it. Birds, animals and insects that will be affected by the construction are asked for forgiveness and prayers are said to them asking that they locate to new homes.

The *shilanyas* ceremony features the *garbhadana* or *garbhanyasa* ritual which involves placing into the foundation a ceremonial copper pot, containing nine types of precious stones, several metals, minerals, herbs and soils symbolizing creation and prosperity.

This auspicious pot is placed at the *brahmasthanam*, above which the *garbhagruha* will be built. The *garbhadana* ritual invites the soul of the mandir to enter within the building confines.

The pot represents the roots of the 'mandir tree'; and the icon its sap. The four walls around the icon represent the branches spreading around. The structure of the *vimana* rises above it in a series of tiers. The roof resting over the walls is called *kapota*, meaning where the doves rest. The imagery suggested is that of a tree with birds perched on its branches. The sanctum is thus a model of a growing tree.

A stone slab (*adhar* or *kurma shila*) is then placed over the spot where the copper pot is buried. Over this slab will rise the

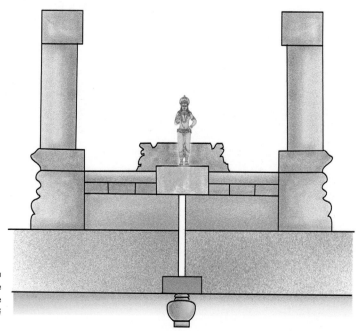

Diagram of the link between the *nidhi kumbha* in the foundation pit and the consecrated *murti*

foundation for installing the *murti*. The copper pot signifies the womb and the icon the life arising out of it. The sanctum constructed around it is the body.

Hewn stones or bricks are then laid in the foundation pointing in the eight cardinal directions.

There are several variations of the *shilanyas* ceremony and the components placed in the foundations vary. In one variation the following components are placed:

Nidhi kumbha: This is a pot made of granite stone or copper and filled with precious stones, gold and other gems. A small stone or metal *kurma* (turtle) is also placed in the pot. Since, in the Purans, the Kurma avatar is described as supporting the earth. The *nidhi kumbha* is placed into the ground while chanting the particular mantra of the deity.

Adhar or *kurma shila:* A base stone with carvings of nine water-related life forms and symbols is placed on top of the *nidhi kumbha*. The central carving is of a *kurma*.

Yoga-nala: This is a hollow copper tube connecting the *kurma* on the *adhar shila* with the *pith*, which is a stone at the level of the ground floor of the *garbhagruha*. The top of the *yoga-nala* is closed temporarily during construction to avoid entry of dirt, insects, etc.

Pith: This is a square stone with measurements depending on

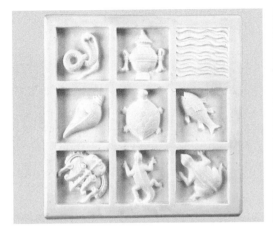

the size of the *murti*. At the bottom of the *pith* there is a hole for attaching the *yoga-nala*. Similarly, at its top there is a square cavity to join the base of the *murti*.

The *bhumipujan* and *shilanyas* ceremonies express: (1) a clear understanding that the environment to be changed is not the exclusive property of humans, but is also home to other life forms and (2) an awareness that nature is a complex dynamic ecosystem created by God in which man must live harmoniously.

MURTI-PRATISHTHA CEREMONY

At the hands of a sculptor a stone becomes a statue and when the divine life-force is infused in the statue by a spiritually enlightened sadhu it becomes a *murti* of God. This spiritual ceremony is termed the *murti-pratishtha* or *pran-pratishtha* – image consecration ceremony. To infuse the divine life-force into a statue means praying to God to reside in the statue to accept the devotion and prayers that will be offered.

During the *murti-pratishtha* ceremony, which ideally should be performed at the hands of a Satpurush (God-realized Sadhu), Vedic mantras are sung and God is invoked to fully reside in the statue.

Just as a battery is charged with an electric current to make it a storehouse of energy, at the hands of a Satpurush, together with the chanting of Vedic mantras, the statue becomes a storehouse of divine energy. Through the consecrated *murti* devotees become inspired with pure thoughts.

When a *murti* is completed, there are special consecration rites which take place. First, the *murti* is purified with a variety of ritually pure sacraments, such as *darbha* grass, honey and ghee. Then

by a rite called *nyas*, literally meaning 'touching', various deities are established in different parts of the *murti*: Brahma in the chest, Indra in the hand, Surya in eyes, the directional guardians in the ear, and so on. Thus, a particular *murti* is symbolically inhabited by a number of deities. Finally, *pran* the 'breath of life', is infused into the *murti* in the central rite called *pran-pratishtha*, 'establishing the breath of life'. The eyes of the *murti* are then symbolically opened using a golden needle-tip dipped in honey and ghee. Thereafter, a mirror is placed before the *murti* to accept the initial vision of the consecrated deity.

After the *murti-pratishtha* ceremony the statue is no longer lifeless, but becomes a living personality in whom a spiritual aspirant experiences God.

PATOTSAV

Every year, on the anniversary of the *murti-pratishtha* ceremony, the *patotsav* ceremony is performed. This involves performing a Vedic *mahapuja* ceremony and its purpose is to reawaken within spiritual seekers an awareness that God manifests in the *murtis* and of the necessity to offer sincere devotion and service for one's spiritual progress.

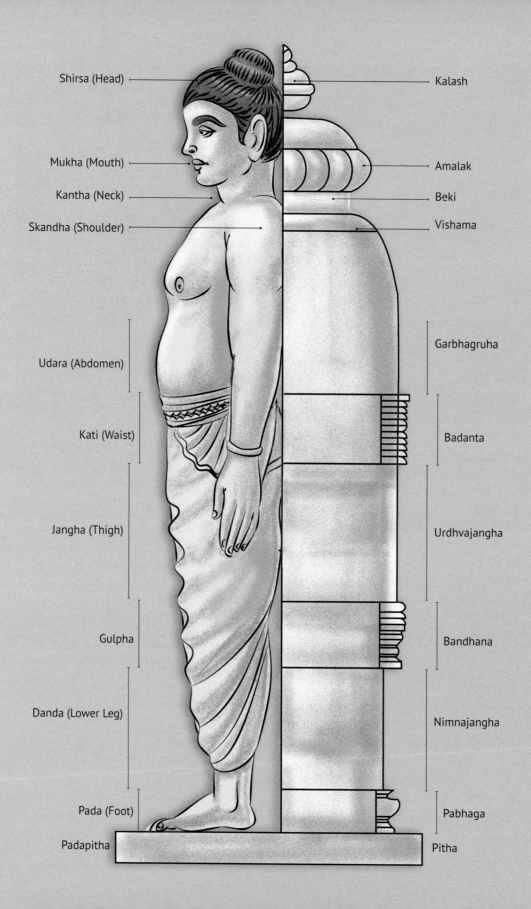

Shirsa (Head)

Mukha (Mouth)

Kantha (Neck)

Skandha (Shoulder)

Udara (Abdomen)

Kati (Waist)

Jangha (Thigh)

Gulpha

Danda (Lower Leg)

Pada (Foot)

Padapitha

Kalash

Amalak

Beki

Vishama

Garbhagruha

Badanta

Urdhvajangha

Bandhana

Nimnajangha

Pabhaga

Pitha

18

Concepts Associated with the Mandir

"The architecture of the Hindu mandir symbolically represents the quest for *moksha*.... For this purpose certain notions are associated with the very forms and materials of the building. Paramount is the identification of the divinity with the fabric of the mandir, or, from another point of view, the identification of the form of the universe [for example, the cosmic mountain] with that of the mandir. Such an identification is achieved through the form and meaning of those architectural elements that are considered fundamental to the mandir."[i]

The various constituent parts of the mandir have been described in previous chapters and from this emerges the view that the Hindu mandir is the home of the deity. The interior darkness of the *garbhagruha* (sanctum sanctorum), illuminated by a dim burning of lights inside, suggests beautifully the idea of mystery that envelopes the universe and the spirit that moves behind the veil of mystery.

The mandir is not only a home of God but the structure of the mandir represents his human form.

Horizontally, the symbolism of the mandir suggests that the *garbhagruha* represents the head, the *antarala* (passage which leads to the main *mandap*) is the neck, the main *mandap* is the torso, the *prakaras* (surrounding walls) are the hands, the *ardhamandap* is the

---

i. George Michell, *The Hindu Temple*, (London: Elek Books Limited, 1977) p.76.

Facing page:
Diagram depicting the relationship between a mandir and the body of God, as described in the Shilparatnakosha

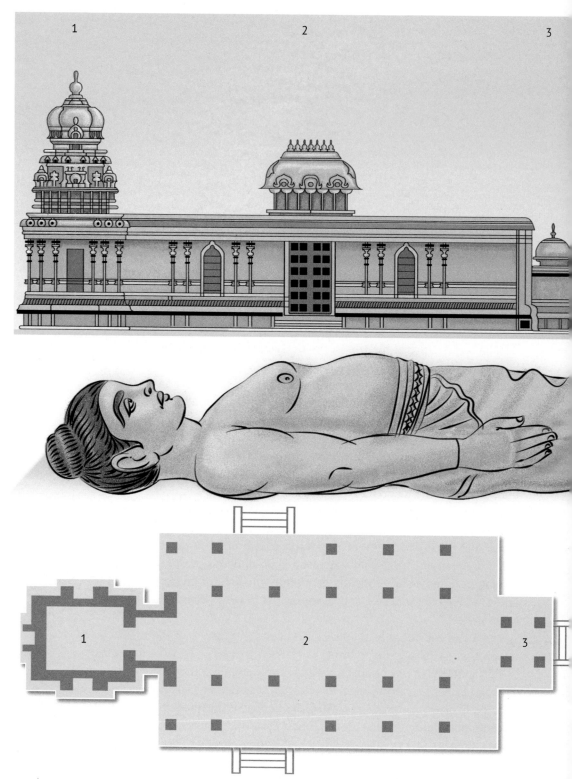

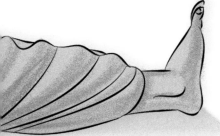

Horizontal Relationship Between Mandir and Body of God

Side (above) and plan (bottom) views of a mandir showing the correlation of various elements to the body of God:

1. Garbhagruha
2. Mandap with pillars
3. Ardhamandap
4. Dhvajasthambha
5. Balipith
6. Gopuram or gate

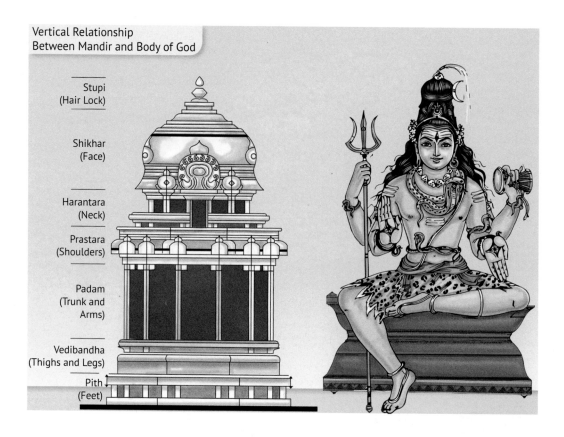

Stupi
(Hair Lock)

Shikhar
(Face)

Harantara
(Neck)

Prastara
(Shoulders)

Padam
(Trunk and
Arms)

Vedibandha
(Thighs and Legs)

Pith
(Feet)

knees and the *gopuram* is the feet of the deity. Vertically, the *pith* represents the feet, *vedibandha* the legs, *padam* (walls) the trunk and arms, *prastara* the shoulders, *hara* the neck, *shikhar* the face, and *stupi* (finial) the tuft of hair (*shikha*).

This concept of the mandir as the body of God is presented in the *Agni Puran*, *Hayshirsha Panchratra* and *Shilparatna* texts.

In addition, when a devotee enters the mandir, his progress through the pavilions to reach the sanctum is also symbolic. It represents the phases of progress in a man's journey towards the divine. On reaching the main gateway, a worshipper first bends down and touches the threshold before crossing it. This marks the transition from the world of the profane to the world of God. Entering the gateway, he is greeted by a host of figures on the outer walls – representing the outward and diverse concerns of man.

As he proceeds, the familiar mythological themes, carved on the walls focus his mind. The pavilion and vestibule near the sanctum are restrained in sculptural details and decorations; these simpler motifs and the prevailing semi-darkness help the worshipper to put aside distractions to focus his attention on the sanctum. The moonstone (semi-circular stone) between the *garbhagruha* and *antarala* symbolizes the interface between the profane and divine. Finally the shrine, devoid of any ornamentation, and with its plainly adorned entrance, leads the devotee further to tranquility, to fulfilment and to the presence of God.

The mandir also represents the subtle body with the seven psychic centres or *chakras*. In the mandir structure, the *brahmarandra* is represented in the part erected on top of the sanctum. The flat roof (*kapota*) of the sanctum is overlaid by a single square stone slab known in the texts as *brahmarandra-shila* (the stone denoting the upper passage of life). The sanctum is viewed as the head; and right on top of the head is the passage through which the currents of life ascend to the tower through this stone slab.

Interestingly, the *kalash* placed on top of the *vimana* is not embedded into the structure with mortar or cement. It is, in fact, placed in position by a hollow rod that juts out of the centre of the tower and runs through the *kalash*. The hollow tube represents the central channel of energy, the *shushumna,* that connects to the *sahasra*, the seat of consciousness, through the *brahmarandra*.

In all classical styles, the mandir towers resemble mountain peaks and the cellas inside, where the *murtis* are kept, resemble caverns. The finials at the top, pointing toward the sky, are aligned with the image inside to signify the sending down of the divine spirit.

Man, from the beginning of his existence, has acknowledged the existence of a superior power to whom he should offer worship. This resulted in shrines and worship rituals. Through the ages the forms of these places and the manner of worship have evolved, but the underlying sentiments have remained.

The mandir and the sculpture upon it represent the cosmos and its eternal harmony. The mandir is conceived as the cosmos in miniature. The mandir is seen as a link between man and god; and between the mundane and the ideal.

19

Mandir Function

The soul of the mandir is the enshrined image – the *murti*. To the faithful and devout the *murti* speaks, laughs, amuses, blesses, accepts.... Unspeaking and lifeless to the unbeliever, the *murti* has for aeons been the epicentre of life for countless millions. Understanding the nature and truth of *murti* worship requires a level of spiritual consciousness. Dry logic and a closed mind are a hindrance.

The function of mandirs is to provide a conducive environment in which to offer both personal and collective bhakti, or worship. The inner sanctum of the mandir is where devotees go to meditate, pray and offer their devotion. Away from the noise and confusion of the material world, amid the sanctified silence, such devotion to God leads to inner transformation of the devotee and purification of the soul.

Many Hindus will include a visit to the mandir for darshan of the *murtis* as part of their daily routine. They will often try to attend either the main morning or evening *arti*. They will participate in the worship rituals and ceremonies performed daily or on special celebratory days.

Hindus practice various devotion traditions, which help them to experience the divine. This is the functional aspect of mandirs. It represents the practical day-to-day use of mandirs in preparing individuals and communities to face the challenges of daily life. Sparing time from a busy daily schedule is only possible because of their faith. Engaging in such devotion strengthens the faith of devotees and they come closer to God.

Facing page:
Devotees throughout the world regularly visit mandirs to participate in and observe a variety of devotional acts. These serve to strengthen their bond with God and grant them an experience of profound inner peace

(Photo courtesy: ISKCON)

A devotee engaged in the darshan of the *murtis*

DARSHAN: SEEING AND RECEIVING

Darshan means 'seeing'. When Hindus go to a mandir, they do not commonly say, "I am going to worship," but rather, "I am going for darshan." They go to 'see' the *murti* of the deity present in the sanctum of the mandir, and they go especially at those times of the day when the *murti* is most beautifully adorned with splendid garments, ornaments and fresh flowers, and when the curtain is drawn back so that the *murti* is fully visible. The central act of Hindu worship, from the point of view of the lay person, is to stand in the presence of the deity and to behold the *murti* with one's own eyes, to see and be seen by the deity.

Darshan is sometimes translated as the 'auspicious sight' of the divine. Since, in Hindu understanding, the deity is present in the *murti,* so beholding the *murti* is an act of worship, and through the eyes of the *murti* one gains the blessings of the divine.

The prominence of the eyes of Hindu divine *murtis* conveys that it is not only the worshipper who sees the deity, but that the deity sees the worshipper as well. The contact between devotee and deity is exchanged through the eyes. Darshan is the receiving of grace through the act of looking upon the divine. The sight of the divine lifts the spirit and creates inner peace and joy.

Devotees offer *dandvats* (prostrations) to the *murtis* of God as a mark of surrender at his holy feet

Through darshan, it is not only vision that is refined, but the other senses as well are focused, ever more sharply, on God. And once they habituate to focus on God the senses lose their attraction for the material world.

DANDVAT: PROSTRATION

Another form of devotion to God involving physical effort is 'dandvat', or prostration. It is a symbol of complete surrenderance to God. When performing a *dandvat* the following parts of the body touch the floor and are focused on God to symbolize submission to him: forehead, nose, chest, hands, legs, mind, vision (eyes) and speech (mouth). This is known as a 'sashtang dandvat'. The name of God is chanted while performing *dandvats*.

PRADAKSHINA: CIRCUMAMBULATING THE MURTI

Circumambulation *(pradakshina)* is a devotion rite involving walking in a clockwise direction around the *garbhagruha*. Many mandirs have ambulatory passageways around the sanctum in which *pradakshinas* are performed. The sacred *murti* housed in the sanctum is the focus.

It is performed to symbolize that God is the centrepoint of one's

Devotees perform *pradakshina* (circumambulation) in recognition that God is the focal point of life and everything revolves around him

life. It also represents the performance of a pilgrimage around the 68 holy places of pilgrimage. While performing *pradakshina* one should turn the rosary, chant the name of God and visualize the presiding deity. Therefore, performing *pradakshinas* with full concentration on the deity gives great solace to an ardent devotee.

Circumambulation is regarded as so important that the shastras state, "With every step whilst performing *pradakshina* one is granted the merit of an Ashvamedha Yagna."

ARTI

The *arti* is the foremost of Hindu prayer rituals. At the time of *arti* the mandir is filled with the faithful, eager for God's darshan. The *arti* is a prayer of humility, gratefulness and enlightenment during which the devotee loses himself in God's form, forgetting the trials and tribulations of life.

The *arti* arose from the act of darshan of the *murti*. The windowless, cave-like *garbhagruha* – sanctum – in ancient mandirs had limited access to natural light. So, to facilitate darshan, the *murti* was dimly illuminated by small lamps. At certain times when many devotees gathered a lamp would be held by the priest close to the deity's hands, feet, head, etc. in a circuitous route enabling the

Performing *arti* focuses one's mind on the supreme glory of God and inspires one towards spiritual enlightenment

gathered devotees to have darshan of the complete *murti* – albeit in parts. Times were fixed that were convenient for most people. Over the years hymns, bells and drums were added to the rites.

The *arti* is performed using lighted wicks placed in special holders. This setup is also known as 'arti'. The *arti* is rotated in a clockwise direction illuminating the deity. Hymns describing the glory of God are sung to the accompaniment of drums and bells.

At the completion of the *arti*, each devotee passes his open palms over the lamps and touches his fingers to his forehead in reverence. Behind this seemingly simple rite is a humble symbolism and acceptance that 'the lamp which enabled me to have God's darshan from divine feet to beautiful face, which helped me to become one with God and let me offer my devotion – to such a lamp (*arti*) I give thanks and honour'.

HINDU WORSHIP OF THE MURTI

The *murti* is the real embodiment of the deity and is charged with the presence of God.

Since the *murti* is a form of God, it facilitates and enhances the close relationship of the worshipper and God and makes possible the deepest outpouring of emotions in worship.

The consecrated deities in the mandir are worshipped with great affection. They are bathed and adorned daily, offered food and other forms of devotion, and cared for as one would attend to a living person

Thus, the *murti* is awakened in the morning, honoured with incense and prayer, dressed, adorned and fed. Throughout the day, other such rites appropriate to the time of day are performed until, finally, the deity is put to bed in the evening.

For Hindus, the human acts of devotion are the gestures of humility with which a servant approaches his master. In addition to bowing, kneeling, prostrating and touching the feet, Hindus utilize the entire range of intimate and ordinary domestic acts as an important part of ritual. So, Hindu worship involves not only rituals of honour but also rituals of affection which enable interaction with the *murti*.

The general term for rites of worship and honour is *puja*. This consists of elaborate forms of worship performed in the home by the householder and in the mandir by special priests called pujaris. These rites involve the presentation of articles of worship, called *upchars*, to the deity. The *upchars* include food, water, fresh flowers, sandalwood paste, incense, garments and ornaments. In addition, waving of the fan and flywhisk is also considered as an *upchar*.

The deity is honoured with fruits and flowers because they are the most beautiful offerings that all people, even the poor, can afford. We offer worship with these particular gestures of reverence

Celebration of Ganesh Chaturthi at a mandir in Rajasthan. Such festivals are celebrated throughout the year with great pomp, devotion and enthusiasm.

because these are the gestures of honour and devotion we know best. Whisking away the flies and offering a drink of water are devotional acts and not God's necessity.

Hindu worship, therefore, is certainly not an occasion for yogic withdrawing of the senses 'as a tortoise withdraws its limbs', but it is, in fact, an occasion directing the senses towards the divine.

It is this direct worship of God that forms the focal point of the religious activities performed in the Hindu mandir.

Some forms of worship that take place in the mandir are more congregational in character. For example, public performances of devotional singing and the recitals of sacred texts and their explanations by learned priests. Other ceremonies occur at regular intervals and are sometimes treated as festivals.

Devotees are encouraged to visit the mandir daily and offer worship and also learn spiritual wisdom by listening to the narration of shastras and their expositions.

From the moment the Vedic rites are completed and a statue or painting of the deity is consecrated God manifests through the *murti* in all his glory and grace. He accepts various devotions. He listens to prayers and woes. He is at once a confidante and giver of blessings.

Youths enjoy the colourful Pushpadolotsav celebrations, BAPS Shri Swaminarayan Mandir, Ahmedabad, Gujarat

Through the *murti* the eye is taught to see God and not to seek God. The first lesson received at the sanctum is to be applied everywhere. See God in everything!

Thus, worship of God through belief in his presence in a *murti* is considered to be one of the foremost aids to spiritual realization in Hinduism.

FESTIVALS

Festivals – *utsavs* – are an important and integral part of mandir worship. One of the most significant aspects of worship in a mandir is its collective character, since festivals encourage participation. They are occasions when all the devotees, regardless of their status in the community, enthusiastically and willingly participate. Festivals help in binding the community together. The pomp, spectacle and splendour of festivals are the expressions of a community's joy, exuberance, devotion and pride, and reflect a community's cohesiveness. These festivals provide an opportunity for youngsters to observe, learn and enjoy the traditions and to actively participate in them. Popular festivals celebrated in mandirs throughout the year include: Uttarayan (January), Vasant Panchmi, Shivratri (January-February), Holi-Dhuleti (March), Ram Navmi, Swaminarayan Jayanti

Arti during the Swaminarayan Jayanti celebration, BAPS Shri Swaminarayan Mandir, Ahmedabad, Gujarat

(March-April), Rath Yatra, Guru Punam (July), Hindola Utsav (July-August) Raksha Bandhan, Janmashtmi (August), Ganesh Chaturthi, Jal-Jhilani Ekadashi (August-September), Dashera, Sharad Punam, Diwali, Annakut (October-November).

To young and old alike they impart an experience of real inner peace and joy.

PROCESSIONS

Mandir processions, which take place regularly in many mandirs, express the radiating presence of the deity. They confirm, in ritual terms, the essential unity of the sacred space with the worldly space around.

During processions, the deity leaves the sanctum and becomes approachable to all. The abstract, all-encompassing reality is given a form that one can relate to and approach, a human form.

DISCOURSES

In the mandir assembly hall devotees listen to the simple and straightforward discourses relating to Brahman and Parabrahman from spiritually experienced and learned sadhus. They gain strength to advance in their spiritual endeavours to realize

Just as a ruler may visit his subjects, the *murtis* are taken on a procession in the mandir grounds, and sometimes outside to enable the faithful to enjoy his darshan and receive blessings

God. Instructive episodes inspire and pacify them. They obtain guidance for practicing spirituality in daily life and solutions to the various problems related to daily life. They gain a fresh insight, becoming aware of the importance of following the scriptural tenets. Discourses in the mandirs serve to clarify and strengthen understanding of spiritual concepts and consolidate faith.

In BAPS Swaminarayan mandirs, there are separate weekly satsang assemblies according to age. This enables the transmission of spiritual messages and tradtions in a manner suitable for and readily understood by children, teenagers and youths. Through such arrangements the youngsters first learn and then teach others. This facilitates the continuous transmission of traditions and values to successive generations.

Thus, a visit to the mandir aids devotees of all ages in their quest for realizing God. They are refreshed with vigour to pursue their devotional practices.

So, a mandir is not just a great work of architecture and sculpture, but is also a special centre to infuse purity and instill values in man, and to satisfy his spiritual needs.

A mandir helps a person gain physically, mentally and spiritually with the ultimate aim of enriching and enlightening the soul,

Pilgrimages reflect the faith of the faithful since many challenges have to be faced. Here, devotees undertake the energy-sapping climb up Mt. Girnar in Junagadh, Gujarat, for darshan of the Dattatreya Mandir

nurturing it to evolve to the highest spiritual state – Brahmic consciousness.

TIRTHYATRA: PILGRIMAGE

The divine presence of God in a duly consecrated mandir has been a constant source of spiritual inspiration to all faithful visitors to a mandir. As the number of mandirs increased and the glory and inspiring effect of their profound spiritual energy spread, people from near and far pilgrimaged to mandirs to experience and personally benefit from the spiritual vibrations. In times past, even when the only reliable and easily available mode of transport was to walk, countless would regularly undertake pilgrimages to far off places. Young or old, healthy or ill, rich or poor, all would tolerate the inevitable difficulties of journeying, and the lack of infrastructure and amenities. This again represented their faith in God and the desire to experience the divinity of mandirs.

After reaching the mandir *tirth*, the devotees will often engage in a special worship ceremony, sometimes even tonsuring their head as a mark of their faith.

In today's modern age, better facilities are available to aid these pilgrimages and millions of devout Hindus and their families from

Above and facing page:
Ghar Mandir – a home shrine enables families to serve and continually experience the presence of God in their daily lives

all over the world undertake pilgrimages every year. To meet the cost of these pilgrimages, they will save and sacrifice over a long period. Such is their deep desire to complete these pilgrimages.

Some of the more famous mandirs to which Hindus pilgrimage include: Tirupati, Amarnath, Sabarimala, Badrinath, Kedarnath, Gangotri, Yamunotri, Vaishno Devi, Somnath, Rameshwaram, Jagannathpuri, and others.

GHAR MANDIRS: DOMESTIC SACRED SPACE

In addition to the public mandirs, Hindus of all denominations, according to their individual means and faith, reserve a place for a shrine in their homes, where family members engage in individual or shared prayer or meditation. From just a plain photo placed in a wall recess to elaborately carved marble or wood mandirs in large rooms, each family seeks to feel the presence of God in their home. These home shrines (*ghar* mandirs) provide all family members a constant reminder of the central role of faith in God in their lives. Each will offer personal worship and the family will gather at least once daily for *arti* in the home shrine. The influence of family members, old or young, is often a starting point for spiritual practices and may inspire service and sacrifice for others. Such

shared worship is a good basis for strenghtening family unity and transmission of traditions.

Also, as part of the daily worship routine in the home, the deities will be offered the meals prepared for the family and only then will everyone partake of the sanctified food.

ATMA MANDIRS: PERSONAL SACRED SPACE

The ultimate aim of mandirs – public and home – is to awaken and feel the presence of God within the *atma* (soul). Through the variety of worship, rituals, ceremonies, celebrations and other endeavours, Hindus strive to experience the highest reward of their faith and devotion – the eternal bliss of God. In fact, despite all attention given to the physically visible public and home mandirs, in the final analysis, all that really matters is the spiritual state of the person, for this will determine his destiny.

For Hindus, every aspect of life, whether spiritual or secular, is a means towards consolidating faith in God and achieving *moksha* for the *atma* housed in this temporary human frame.

20

BAPS Swaminarayan Mandirs

The preceding chapters have revealed the history and form of the Hindu mandir. The tradition of building such elaborate stone mandirs has been sustained throughout India to the present day.

In Gujarat, Bhagwan Swaminarayan (1781-1830), founder of the Swaminarayan Sampradaya, built such mandirs in Ahmedabad (1822), Bhuj (1823), Vartal (1824), Dholera (1826), Junagadh (1828) and Gadhada (1829). These mandirs were built in the *nagara* style and set the precedence for the style of future traditional mandirs built in the Sampradaya.

His Holiness Shastriji Maharaj (1865-1951), the third spiritual successor of Bhagwan Swaminarayan and founder of the Bochasanwasi Shri Akshar Purushottam Swaminarayan Sanstha (BAPS), revived the tradition of building such elegant mandirs in the style adopted by Bhagwan Swaminarayan. Shastriji Maharaj built mandirs in Bochasan (1907), Sarangpur (1916), Gondal (1934), Atladra (1945) and Gadhada (1951). His successor, His Holiness Yogiji Maharaj (1892-1971), built mandirs in Ahmedabad (1962) and Bhadra (1969).

Continuing this tradition begun by Bhagwan Swaminarayan, the present guru of BAPS, His Holiness Pramukh Swami Maharaj, has inspired over 30 such traditional mandirs, known in the *sampradaya* as *shikharbaddha* mandirs. He has also inspired over 1,000 mandirs, small and large, built of modern day building materials like concrete, steel and glass. These are known in the *sampradaya* as *hari* mandirs.

For many decades, Hindus have migrated to lands outside India and are among the largest ethnic communities in some countries.

Facing page:
BAPS Shri Swaminarayan
Mandir, Houston, Texas, USA

Left: Bhagwan Swaminarayan (1781-1830), founder of the Swaminarayan Sampradaya

Right: His Holiness Shastriji Maharaj (1865-1951), third spiritual successor of Bhagwan Swaminarayan; established BAPS Swaminarayan Sanstha in 1907

They migrate for education, employment and entrepreneurial purposes in the hope of economic and other gains. They are respected by the host countries as among the most peaceful, productive and law-abiding communities. Over the years, they have contributed immensely to the economic growth, cultural diversity and spiritual mosaic of many countries.

Depending on local requirements and resources, Hindus of many denominations have established mandirs of various forms to serve their communities. As the Hindus become more affluent they are able to build traditional style mandirs outside India.

Inspired by Pramukh Swami Maharaj, BAPS has built such traditional stone mandirs outside India in the UK and USA. In addition, he has inspired the grand Swaminarayan Akshardham complexes in Gandhinagar, Gujarat, and New Delhi. At the heart of these two complexes are the grand, magnificent mandirs. A third such mandir and complex is under construction in Robbinsville, New Jersey, USA.

The following pages show some of the mandirs built by Bhagwan Swaminarayan, mandirs built by Shastriji Maharaj and a detailed line drawing depicting the various architectural elements of a typical BAPS mandir, so that visitors can identify these common components and better appreciate the traditions of Hindu mandir architecture continued by the BAPS Swaminarayan Sanstha. The

chapter concludes with a series of photographs of the Swaminarayan Akshardham mandirs in New Delhi and Gandhinagar, various other BAPS mandirs and close-up views of various elements demonstrating the variety, beauty, intricacy and majesty of the carvings and components that comprise BAPS mandirs. The latter photos are categorized into sections: *shikhar* (pinnacle), external *ghummat* (dome), *sthambha* (pillar), *jharukho* (balcony), *mandovar* (rear *garbhagruha* wall), internal *ghummat* (dome), ceiling, *dwarshakh* (doorframe), *kakshasan* (seat), interior views, exterior views, sculptures and *parikrama* (circumambulatory path). Where appropriate, the first photo of each section is labelled to aid the identification of common structural elements.

Side View of a Typical BAPS Mandir

1. Samran
2. Peti
3. Dasho
4. Janghi
5. Kanpith
6. Jagati

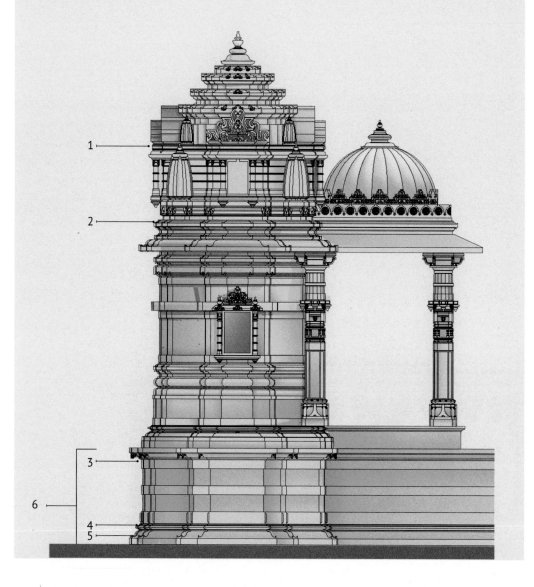

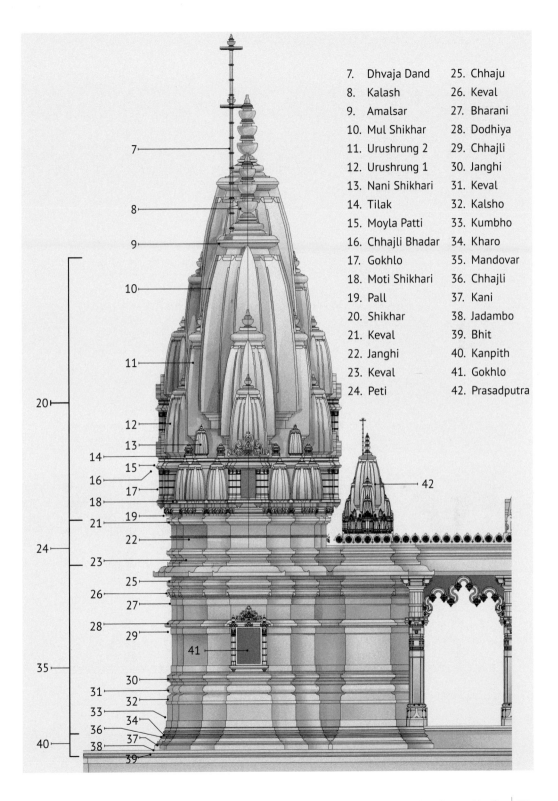

7. Dhvaja Dand
8. Kalash
9. Amalsar
10. Mul Shikhar
11. Urushrung 2
12. Urushrung 1
13. Nani Shikhari
14. Tilak
15. Moyla Patti
16. Chhajli Bhadar
17. Gokhlo
18. Moti Shikhari
19. Pall
20. Shikhar
21. Keval
22. Janghi
23. Keval
24. Peti

25. Chhaju
26. Keval
27. Bharani
28. Dodhiya
29. Chhajli
30. Janghi
31. Keval
32. Kalsho
33. Kumbho
34. Kharo
35. Mandovar
36. Chhajli
37. Kani
38. Jadambo
39. Bhit
40. Kanpith
41. Gokhlo
42. Prasadputra

43. Kalash
44. Amalsar
45. Chandrash
46. Ghummati
47. Ghummat

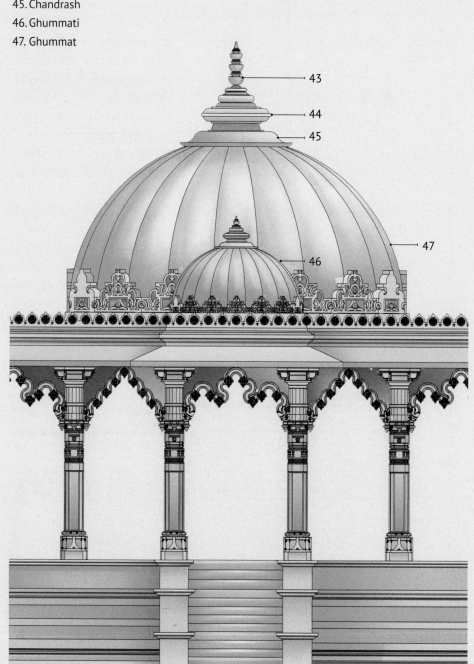

43

44

45

47

46

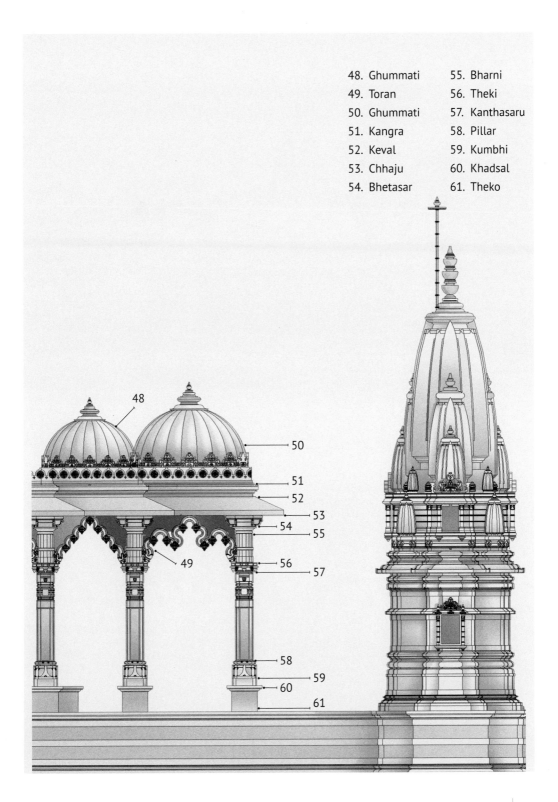

48. Ghummati
49. Toran
50. Ghummati
51. Kangra
52. Keval
53. Chhaju
54. Bhetasar

55. Bharni
56. Theki
57. Kanthasaru
58. Pillar
59. Kumbhi
60. Khadsal
61. Theko

Mandirs Built by Bhagwan Swaminarayan

Shri Swaminarayan Mandir, Ahmedabad, 1822

Shri Swaminarayan Mandir, Dholera, 1826

Shri Swaminarayan Mandir, Junagadh, 1828

Shri Swaminarayan Mandir, Gadhada, 1829

BAPS Shri Swaminarayan Mandir, Bochasan, 1907

BAPS Shri Swaminarayan Mandir, Sarangpur, 1916

BAPS Shri Swaminarayan Mandir, Gondal, 1934

BAPS Shri Swaminarayan Mandir, Gadhada, built by Shastriji
Maharaj and consecrated by Yogiji Maharaj in 1951

Mandirs Built by Pramukh Swami Maharaj

BAPS Swaminarayan Akshardham, New Delhi, 2005

BAPS Swaminarayan Akshardham, Gandhinagar, 1992

BAPS Shri Swaminarayan Mandir, London, 1995

BAPS Shri Swaminarayan Mandir, Toronto, 2007

BAPS Shri Swaminarayan Mandir, Bhadra, 2010

Kalabo

Jhivha

Mul Shikhar

Urushrung 2

Urushrung 1

Tilak

Gavaksha

Paychat Shikhari

Prasadputra

Shikharpeti

Chicago, IL, USA

Mahuva, Gujarat, India

Chicago, IL, USA

Bodeli, Gujarat, India

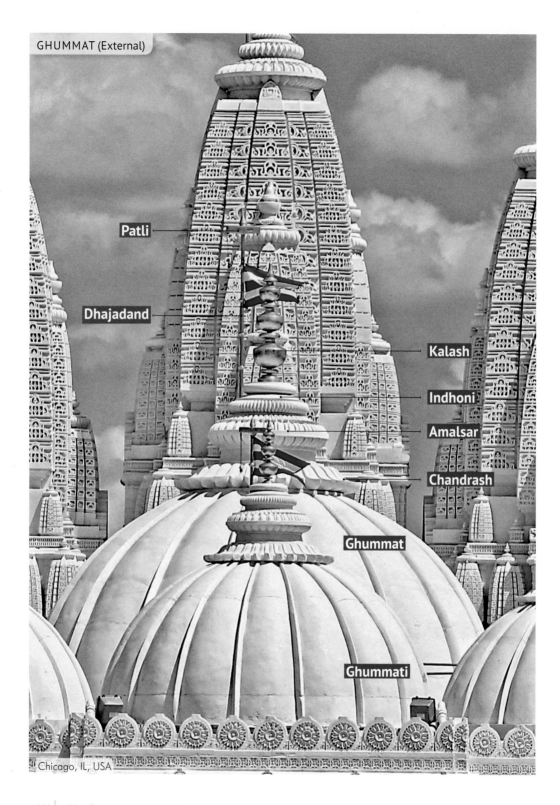

GHUMMAT (External)

Patli

Dhajadand

Kalash

Indhoni

Amalsar

Chandrash

Ghummat

Ghummati

Chicago, IL, USA

Himmatnagar, Gujarat, India

Los Angeles, CA, USA

Atlanta, GA, USA

STHAMBHA

Bhetasaro

Bharni

Toran

Kanthasaru

Bharni

Theki

Sthambha

Kumbhi

Daso

Theko

Khadsal

Nagpur, Maharashtra, India

Houston, TX, USA

JHARUKHO

Kapchar

Keval
Chhajli

Thambhli

Kakshasan

Asanpatt

Vedika

Rajsen

Rekha

Kanpith

Padhro

Bhit

Bhadra

Nagpur, Maharashtra, India

Selvas, Gujarat, India

MANDOVAR

Keval 2

Keval 1

Bharni

Galato

Dodhiyo

Janghi

Daso

Machi

Keval 1

Kalasho

Kumbho

Kharo

Kanpith

Bhit

Kolkata, West Bengal, India

Bhadra, Gujarat, India

Los Angeles, CA, USA

GHUMMAT (Internal)

Keystone

Sei

Beam

Kolkata, West Bengal, India

Robbinsville, NJ, USA

Los Angeles, CA, USA

Toronto, ON, Canada

Ceiling

Beam

Kanas

Kolkata, West Bengal, India

Los Angeles, CA, USA

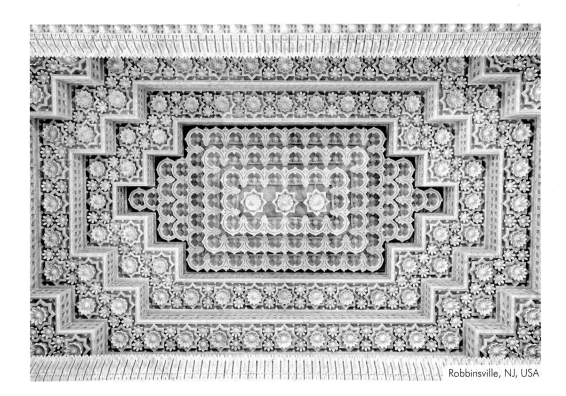

Robbinsville, NJ, USA

Toronto, ON, Canada

DWARSHAKH

Otarang

Dwarshakh

Umbro

Gras

Maanu

Ahmedabad, Gujarat, India

Kakshasan

Asanpatt

Vedika

Rajsen

Chhajli

Jagati Jharukho

Bodeli, Gujarat, India

Los Angeles, CA, USA

London, UK

Kolkata, West Bengal, India

Mahuva, Gujarat, India

Swaminarayan Akshardham, New Delhi, India

Houston, TX, USA

Toronto, ON, Canada

Los Angeles, CA, USA

SCULPTURES

Robbinsville, NJ, USA

Los Angeles, CA, USA

Los Angeles, CA, USA

Robbinsville, NJ, USA

London, UK

Jamngar, Gujarat, India

Swaminarayan Akshardham, New Delhi, India

PARIKRAMA

Kolkata, West Bengal, India

21

MANDIR FAQs

1. What is a mandir?

A mandir is a Hindu place of worship. It is regarded as a 'house of God' and is also considered as representing the whole cosmos in miniature form. It can vary in size from a small shrine to a large, elaborate structure. It is a place where the mind is pacified and one can offer devotion and service to God.

A mandir is regarded as holy because it is constructed according to the sacred *vastushastra* principles and the *murtis* of deities are enshrined in accordance with sacred consecration rituals which invoke the presence of God in the *murtis* to accept the devotion and service of all. It is holy since it allows people to meet the divine, and is a place where holy actions and events take place.

2. How did mandirs evolve? How many mandirs are there in India?

In later Vedic times (2700-1750 BCE), *murtis* of dieties were made and enshrined in simple mandirs built of perishable materials such as clay, bricks, wood and bamboo. In India, it is believed that Buddhists were the first to develop religious architecute in the form of *chaitya* halls (rectangular buildings with a semi-circular wall behind a mini-stupa and a vaulted ceiling, usually erected on a high plinth), *viharas* (residence hall, composed of small, square cells surrounding a square or rectangular open-air court) and rock-cut

Facing page:
Illustration of craftsmen sculpting various elements of a mandir

structures. As the Hindu bhakti traditions grew, caves were used as shrines and also rock-cut mandirs were made by chiselling rock until the desired shape was achieved. These early Hindu mandirs were called *rathas*. At the same time, small stone mandirs were built to resemble caves. Then, over time, larger and more ornate mandirs were built, with different regions of India developing variations on the same underlying form.

3. Why build mandirs?

a. It is true that God is omnipresent and permeates the whole of creation. However, his omnipresence is at such a very subtle level that most people are unable to experience it. An analogy will help to understand this: just as a telescope is used to see distant stars and galaxies and a microscope is used to view minuscule things, and even though air is everywhere, we still need a fan to feel it, similarly mandirs facilitate an experience of the divine through the consecrated *murtis*.

b. Mandirs occupy a special place in the hearts of many Hindus who desire to worship God because they remind them of everything that is important, enable them to be close to God, facilitate cleansing of the soul and give an experience of God's divine abode on earth. The mandir also gives a Hindu identity to all devotees.

c. There are so many distractions in life, and thus we need to nourish our spiritual selves and celebrate holy festivals. Mandirs are where we can go to be enriched, encouraged and enlightened. Mandirs give people a lift and feelings of joy when they are confused, afraid or despondent.

d. Mandirs enshrine a particular philosophy. The *murtis* consecrated within serve as a reminder of the beliefs of the that particular tradition. The faith of devotees who adhere to these specific beliefs is strengthened by regular visits to the mandir.

4. How are mandirs useful to society?

a. Every living person possesses both a physical body and a metaphysical soul. So, just as schools, colleges and universities educate the mind, mandirs educate the soul. Mandirs are where spirituality and ethics are learnt to help us become better people. Mandirs teach respect for all, open-mindedness and appreciation, and so foster a more harmonious society.

b. Mandirs nurture religious beliefs and analysis of peer-reviewed scientific literature reveals that religious belief is associated, to varying degrees, with positive mental health outcomes, including: decreased depression, anxiety and suicide risk, improved psychological wellbeing and increased life satisfaction.

Mandirs provide opportunities to connect socially with others and secure social support. There is a strong link between social connections and support and good physical and mental health. Research by the famous Blue Zones Project (www.bluezones.com) reveals that one of the nine main factors leading to a longer, happier and healthier life is personal involvement in a faith-based community.

c. Religious belief helps people cope better with stress and serves as an alternative to less healthy coping strategies (e.g., alcohol, smoking, risky sexual behaviours, and criminal and delinquent activities). In particular, this appears to offer protection during teenage and adolescent years.

d. Attendance at places of worship and other forms of religious involvement keeps people physically active, which in turn reduces the risk of disability.

e. The mandir serves as a host for a variety of humanitarian activities, which are organized, launched and managed on its premises. It provides resources and manpower for such projects.

f. Historically, in India, mandirs have been a centre for intellectual and artistic life. Mandirs have been the most significant patrons of architecture, sculpture and painting. The greatest architectural projects, the greatest sculptures and paintings of every age have been associated with the construction of mandirs. Also, mandirs have been great patrons of the performing arts. Mandirs supported the performance and teaching of devotional vocal and instrumental music. Mandirs also promoted the tradition of devotional dance. These traditions of music and dance were developed in the mandir and spread out into the wider culture.

g. Mandirs preserve scriptural traditions. It was through the mandirs, where the scriptures were regularly read, studied and discoursed upon, that the public was able to gain regular access to the stories and messages of the the shastras that are the foundation of Hindu culture.

h. Mandirs preserve language, which is the key to unlocking the history and teachings that have been preserved in the shastras. Mandirs have preserved the knowledge of Sanskrit by establishing *pathshalas* (teaching centres) where Sanskrit and the shastras are taught. The mandir's role in the teaching of languages such as Sanskrit and, in mandirs outside of India, Gujarati and Hindi, continues today.

i. An individual's affiliation with the mandir is often family based. The influence of the mandir accompanies him or her into the home. Normally, family members are also involved and influenced by the mandir. This helps to foster unity and intra-family understanding.

The mandir community is itself a family of families. As a result, the environment of the mandir allows one family to mingle with and learn from many other highly functional and cohesive families.

j. Through its natural teachings and activities of prayer and worship, the mandir generates devout faith in God and in fellow man and guides the individual towards spirituality. They mould the character of individuals by endowing basic virtues of humanity such as fidelity, courage, forgiveness, unity, friendship, honesty, humility, tolerance, understanding, patience, charity and universal brotherhood.

Thus, mandirs play an important role in improving society by improving the state of the individual and families.

5. Why spend so much on building big, elaborate mandirs? Why not spend the money on schools, hospitals and other societal needs?

a. Just as no cost or effort is spared in our quest for a perfect home for ourselves and our loved ones, similarly those who love God spare no effort or cost to make the perfect house for God. This has been the sentiment of Hindus for over a millennia. The elaborate features and exquisite carvings of mandirs are simply the physical embodiment of the devotion of the devotees who constructed the mandirs. For centuries, Hindus have had a tradition of building grand mandirs as well as small shrines.

Also, God is the entire creation and the rightful owner of everything that exists. In fact, humans are the earthly occupants of his property, so it is only just that our debt to him is duly acknowledged by building sacred places and worshipping him.

b. Governments everywhere spend millions of dollars on public monuments that have no function other then to be looked at and admired for their architecture. The money to construct such monuments often comes directly from taxpayers. Yet, such massive expenditure on public monuments is accepted and appreciated by all, since, through their architecture and symbolism, such public monuments promote pride in one's country and its values, and thus spread a beneficial social message. In the same way, the architecture of a mandir also promotes a message that is spiritually and socially beneficial. The architecture of the mandir evokes feelings of purity, devotion, faith, wonder at the splendour of God and pride in one's culture.

Moreover, the money spent on mandirs does not come from public funds, but from the donations of devotees who desire to express their devotion to God through the mandir. If society admires wealthy people for the massive mansions and palaces they construct to serve their own personal needs, should not society admire even more, those people from all backgrounds who selflessly donate to the mandir for the socially beneficial messages the mandir promotes.

c. Hospitals, schools and mandirs each play essential roles in maintaining society's physical, mental and spiritual well-being. A hospital is necessary to treat the ill and wounded. A school is necessary to educate the mind of the individual so that he or she may become a successful and productive member of society. However, neither schools nor hospitals can provide the social, cultural, and spiritual benefits given by a mandir. Furthermore, the duty of building schools, hospitals and other necessary infrastructure lies upon the government to whom the citizens pay tax.

Mandirs fuel our faith in God, strengthen our society and teach us to trust one another and to become trustworthy. Schools educate the mind, but who will educate the soul? Hospitals will mend a broken arm, but who will mend a broken heart? Cinemas and arcades will excite the mind, but where will one go for peace of mind? The answer, of course, is mandirs.

d. Much money, resources, time and effort is put into producing movies and other forms of entertainment which may provide pleasure for a short time. However, in the long term, the positive impact of such extravagant expenditure in terms of promoting personal character and social harmony is highly questionable. Whereas, funds used for building mandirs continue to inspire individuals, families and society in positive ways for many years.

e. Many religious organizations do, in fact, build and manage schools and hospitals, and engage in a wide variety of other social activities on a regular basis as part of their spectrum of services to society.

6. Why do people go to a mandir?

a. People may visit mandirs for a variety of mundane reasons: to pray to God for material favours, to gain the support and affection that comes by being part of the faith community, or purely as a habit or tradition inculcated by the culture one is born into.

However, those who seek to experience the bliss of God have a more sublime purpose. They go to mandirs to seek the aura of tranquility that inhabits the place, an aura that has been created through the ages because people have engaged in contemplation, chanting and other devotional activities. One needs such a harmonious atmosphere in order to reinforce one's fluctuating willpower and calm the wavering mind.

b. A personal relationship with God is an individual experience, but it is not a private experience. In fact, God, who is infinite, is best known with the help of a community of worshippers. This is understood through the story of the blind men and the elephant. Each of the men grasped a part of the elephant and described it, but none had the overall picture. Only by combining everyone's view could it be described fully.

Similarly, we are like the blind men and can hardly appreciate the little bit of Divinity revealed to us. Hence, we need more people to describe their part of the 'elephant'.

Thus, meeting together is important to our spiritual growth, and encouragement and guidance from others will help us grow spiritually.

7. What forms of worship are offered by people in a mandir?

a. In a mandir, people gather to pray, perform rituals and

ceremonies, and meditate, either individually or together. They also sing bhajans, listen to spiritual discourses and celebrate festivals to become internally recharged. Such sacred actions link the faithful with their past, enable them to make sense of a sometimes confusing present and to face the unknown future with confidence. Repetition of such sacred actions can help stabilize the inner rhythms which make life human.

b. Human beings are physical beings and express themselves not only through intellectual activities and personal prayer, but by a variety of external gestures.

i. *Pradakshina* (or *parikrama*) – circumambulation. In order to prepare to benefit from darshan of the *murtis*, devotees walk clockwise around the mandir. In this way the mind is prepared by consciously removing all its internal disturbances so that undisturbed communication with God is possible.

ii. Darshan of the *murtis* of God adorned in beautiful clothes, ornaments and garlands is a devotional form of worship. Focused darshan establishes the image of God within and enables recall.

iii. *Arti* is the devotional waving of *divas* before the *murtis* of God. When one either performs or does darshan of the performance of the *arti* and listens to the words of the *arti* being sung, one naturally remembers with devotion, the glory of God. Afterwards, when the *arti* is offered, hands should be passed over the flame, and then over the eyes, forehead and head in one movement to symbolically transfer Divinity within.

iv. *Thal* is the devotional offering of food to the deities. While *thal* is being sung and offered to God, one can imagine oneself personally offering sweet and savoury dishes to God.

v. *Abhishek* is the ritual of pouring water over the *murti* while reciting mantras and prayers for whatever one wishes; it enables worshippers to directly interact with the *murti*.

vi. Bhajans – devotional songs – are sung before the deities to help one remember his divine form, glory and extraordinary deeds.

All of these and many more devotional acts of worship help to enhance one's individual relationship with God and consolidate bhakti.

8. What codes of conduct should be observed in a mandir?

a. Since the mandir is a consecrated building, it should be respected as such by practicing proper conduct and appropriate use. The mandir has been made for God, and for all who seek his darshan and blessings. It has been consecrated for religious purposes and is not for worldly or common uses. It is disrespectful to treat it as a common thing. People show their respect when they visit by wearing respectful clothes, observing appropriate silence, bowing and adhering to specific requests.

b. Our clothes reflect the emphasis we place on worship to God, and they should be in keeping with the dignity of the occasion. Our dress should be clean, proper, chaste and decent. It should not call attention to ourselves because it is showy, sloppy or lewd. When we worship we are actually in the presence of God, and he deserves only our very best behaviour.

c. Before entering the shrine area, visitors are required to take off their shoes. This is an Indian tradition and a sign of respect. It also maintains the purity and cleanliness of the mandir, as this is God's home.

Other religions also require the removal of footwear before entering their holy place.

d. Male-female segregation during worship and other activities in the mandir is important since this enables everyone to focus on the main purpose of visiting the mandir: offering devotion and service to God. As humans, men and women are naturally drawn to each other, but to interact with improper intentions in the presence of God is unacceptable. So, this practice is not to discriminate against any gender, but to emphasize that, as devotees of God, our focus while in the mandir must remain on God.

In the eyes of God, we are all his beloved children – irrespective of caste or creed, class or credentials, wealth or intellect, nationality or gender. However, as fallible human beings, we have yet to attain spiritual perfection. And to attain this perfection, we must rigorously observe the religious disciplines clearly stated in the shastras.

9. What is the significance of *murtis*?

Even though God is omnipresent, we are not able to see him in everything due to our human-centric outlook. So, first, we practice seeing him in at least one image and then slowly expand our vision.

A mandir is usually dedicated to a particular deity. God is present in the *murtis* consecrated in the mandir and accepts the devotion, prayers and service of devotees, as a result of which they gain spiritual merit.

10. Why do people place offerings before the deities?

It is a traditional custom that whenever one approaches a king, one should not go empty handed. Give to him according to one's means because he provides and protects. Since God is the king of all creation, one should recognize one's debt to him and present him with gifts according to one's means.

11. What is the reason for flags on top of the mandir?

A flag (*dhaja*) atop any building denotes the glory of the occupant of that building. So, in a mandir the flag represents the glory of the deity enshrined within. Different denominations use flags of different shapes, sizes and colours.

The flags atop BAPS Swaminarayan mandirs represent the victory of good over evil and are red and white in colour. Red represents devotion and auspiciousness, while white represents purity.

12. What is the reason for ringing a bell during darshan and other rituals?

A bell may be rung as worship begins and even during it to ward off evil spirits and invite devotees to be in the presence of God.

Also, a conch shell may be sounded to assist in concentration while worshipping.

13. What is *prasad*?

Food becomes sacred after it has been offered to the deity, usually before the *arti* ceremony. After that it is called *prasad*. It is often in the form of sweets or cooked food. Visitors are generally offered some, which may be eaten on the premises or taken home.

14. Why do people have a home mandir?

Since ancient times, Hindus have reserved space in their homes for a shrine where the family can honour and worship God. The presence of a home mandir turns the home into a mandir, since daily individual or collective family worship spreads the aura of divinity throughout the home and infuses each member of the family with peace and bliss.

Home mandirs enable children to worship God from their early years, strengthen the family's faith in God, and offer collective prayer for family problems and needs.

Although it is important to visit the local community mandir, it may not be possible to do so every day. Home mandirs facilitate continuity in worship in such circumstances.

15. What activities take place in BAPS mandirs?

BAPS was established by His Holiness Shastriji Maharaj in 1907, based on the Akshar-Purushottam philosophy revealed by Bhagwan Swaminarayan, who emphasized the importance of mandirs in enabling correct theological worship (*upasana*). BAPS mandirs are built with this perspective in mind.

In addition to such worship, the mandir premises are used to strengthen the spirituality of devotees and for activities that contribute to the development of individuals, families and the society.

Spiritual activities include separate weekly assemblies (*sabhas*) for different age groups, and regular seminars and conventions that teach spiritual values and traditions.

Activities that encourage and assist in academic progress, healthy living and personal development are held. Campaigns to raise social awareness of the harmful consequences of smoking, alcohol, and drug and other addictions are conducted.

As a global socio-spiritual Hindu organization, BAPS operates educational institutes, hospitals and free mobile medical clinics, promotes environmental awareness, and provides relief and rehabilitation in the aftermath of natural disasters.

BAPS mandirs, outside India especially, are regularly visited by school, college and university students as part of their studies. Also, groups of tourists from different parts of the world visit these mandirs. During such visits they gain a firsthand experience of the devout and peaceful ambience of the mandir and are able to learn about the fundamental features of Hinduism in general and Swaminarayan Hinduism in particular.

BIBLIOGRAPHY

Acharya, Prasana Kumar. *An Encyclopaedia of Hindu Architecture.* New Delhi: D.K. Publishers, 2001.

Bharne, V. and Krusche, K. *Rediscovering the Hindu Temple: The Sacred Architecture and Urbanism of India.* Cambridge: Cambridge Scholars Publishing, 2012.

Brown, Percy. *Indian Architecture (Buddhist and Hindu Periods).* D.B. Taraporevala (Original from University of Virginia), 1965.

Desai, D. *The Religious Imagery of Khajuraho.* Mumbai: Project for Indian Cultural Studies, 1996.

Gupta, S.P. and Vijayakumar, S. *Temples in India – Origin and Developmental Stages.* New Delhi: Centre for Research and Training in History, Archaeology and Paleo-Environment, 2010.

Hardy, Adam. *Indian Temple Architecture: Form and Transformation.* New Delhi: Indira Gandhi National Centre for the Arts (IGNCA), 1995.

Hardy, Adam. *The Temple Architecture of India.* Chichester: John Wiley & Sons Ltd., 2007.

Kramrisch, Stella. *The Hindu Temple*, Volumes 1 and 2. New Delhi: Motilal Banarsidass, 1976.

Michell, George. *The Hindu Temple: An Introduction to Its Meaning and Form.* London: Elek Book Limited, 1977.

Srinivasan, P.R. . *The Indian Temple Art and Architecture.* India: University of Mysore, 1982.

GLOSSARY

A

abhanga   posture in which body is slightly deflected from the centre at the head or waist with the weight more on one foot.

abhay mudra   right hand raised to shoulder level with palm facing the viewer. This gesture symbolizes that the devotee should remain fearless since the deity will protect.

abhishek   ritual pouring of milk or water over a *murti* as a mark of honour and prayer.

acharya   a teacher, leader or learned person

adhar shila   stone slab placed in the foundations

adhisthana   plinth

alankar   ornamentation

amalak   serrated stone at the top of a *shikhar*

amalsar   see *amalak*

amrut   nectar

andak   a component of a *kalash*

angula   finger

ankush   goad

antarala   intermediate passage between *garbharuha* and *mahamandap*

ardhamandap   a portico or porch

arti   ritual waving of lighted wicks before the *murti* of God as a form of devotion

asana   seat or posture

ashram   stage of life

dikpal   guardians

ashvattha   peepal tree

astik   having faith in God

atibhanga   posture in which body has several bends such that head, torso and limbs are in differing directions

atma   soul

ayudha   emblem

B

balipitha   pedestal for ritual offerings

bara   wall (Orissa)

beki   short cylindrical neck

bhadra   central projection emerging from rear wall

bhanga   flexion or curve

bhogamandap   hall for offerings

bhumi   horizontal sections

bhumi-amalak   *amalak*-shaped stone which demarcates a tier on a *shikhar*

bhumija type of *nagara shikhar*

bhumi pujan ceremony to sanctify the ground

bijpur component of a *kalash*

bilva *Aegle marmalos*. Also known as bael, wood apple and bili. Sacred tree associated with Lord Shiva

brahmasthanam literally, the place of Brahman. It is the central spot of the *garbhagruha*

C

chakra circle, disc; energy point in the subtle body

chakravyuha circular battle formation

chandrashala window

chitra painting

D

daiva a divine being

damaru drum

dandvat prostration

darbha type of sacred grass

deul sanctum/mandir (Orissa)

dhaja flag

dhvaja flag

dhvajasthambha flagpole

diksha initiation

dipasthambha pole on which lighted wicks are placed as lamps

divo lighted wick

dravida South Indian style mandir

dvikuta double-shrined *garbhagruha*

dwarpal gatekeeper or guard in the service of the presiding deity of the mandir

dwarshakh door frame

G

gala name of a moulding in the *vedibandha*

garbhadana/garbhanyasa part of the *shilanyas* ceremony in which a sanctified pot is placed in the ground

garbhagruha sanctum sanctorum

gaumukh water spout on outside wall of *garbhagruha* draining lustral water

gavaksha window

ghata-pallava pot-flower design

ghummat dome

gopuram gate of South Indian mandir

grasmukh the devourer

griva neck

H

harantara   row of miniature shrines

hara   miniature shrine

I

ishanya   north-eastern

J

jagati   base

jangha   wall

jnan   knowledge

jnan mudra   the thumb and index finger of the right hand join to form a circle and touch the heart, with the palm facing inwards. It conveys the message that knowledge (jnan) comes from within

K

kai chan   equal to the distance between the middle finger and the thumb of the extended hand

kai tala   equivalent to the length of the extended hand from the tip of the middle finger to the wrist of that person

kalash   auspicious pot

kalyan mandap   hall for marriage ceremonies

kama   mundane desires

kamandal   water jug

kapota   cornice

karnika   component of a *kalash*

khapuri   skull-like element on a *shikhar*

kirtimukh   lion face

korimandap   intermediate passage between *garbhagruha* and *mahamandap*

kovil   sanctum santorum (Tamil Nadu)

kumuda   a moulding of the *vedibandha*

kurma   turtle made of stone or metal with its head facing the same direction as the deity.

kuta   square

kutina   South Indian spire

L

lata   creeper

latina   type of *nagara shikhar*

ling   symbol of Shiva

M

mahamandap   main hall

mahapuja   special, elaborate worship rituals
mandala   sacred geometric diagram symbolizing the cosmos
mandap   hall
mandovar   outside wall of sanctum sanctorum
manushya   human
marma   point of intersection of lines on the *vastupurush mandala*
mithun   the state of being a couple
moksha   liberation
mudra   hand gesture
mukham   facial length
mula-prasada   sanctum sanctorum
murti-pratishtha   consecration of *murtis*
murti   idol, image

N
nagara   northern style mandir
nairutya   southwest corner
napunsak shila   a stone placed in the foundations during the *shilanyas* ceremony
natya mandapa   dance hall
natyashastra   the texts of the dancing arts
navaranga   main hall in front of *garbhagruha*
nidhi kumbha   sanctified pot placed in the foundations during the *shilanyas* ceremony
nirandhara   no circumambulatory path
nrutya mandap   hall for dance and artistic performances
nyas   purification rite

O
ovu   water spout on outside wall of *garbhagruha* draining lustral water

P
pabhaga   foot portion (Orissa)
padgrahi   component of a kalash
padma pattika   component of a *kalash*
paduka   footwear
paishacha   evil spirit
panchadhatu   alloy of five metals used to make icons: gold, silver, copper, iron, zinc
pancharatha   wall with five projections and recessions from its surface
paramasayika   9 x 9 *vastupurush mandala* grid
patotsav   annual celebration of *murti-pratishtha* date
phamsana   stepped pyramid type of *nagara shikhar*
pitha   base – which may be plain or comprise of several bands of decorative mouldings
   featuring various designs

pradakshina   circumambulation

prakara   enclosure, or boundary, walls

pran   breath of life

pran-pratishtha   consecration of *murtis*

pranala   water spout on outside wall of *garbhagruha* draining lustral water

prasada   sanctum sanctorum

prastara   entablature

pujan   worship

purush   cosmic man

purusharth   endeavour

R

rahumukh   the eclipser

ratha   chariot; also, wall segment

S

sala   miniature rectangular shrine

samabhanga   posture in which the whole body remains straight, unflexed and equally distributed along a central line

sandhara   enclosed circumambulatory path

saptaratha   wall with seven projections and recessions from its surface

shaligram   aniconic *murti* of Vishnu

shayana   reclining

shekhari   type of *nagara shikhar*

shikhar   spire, pinnacle, superstructure

shila   stone

shilanyas vidhi   Vedic foundation stone-laying ceremony

shilpa   sculpture

shilpi   sculptor

sinhasan   throne

skandha   shoulder, a truncated top

smruti   recollection

sopana   staircase

sthambha   pillar, column

sthanaka   standing

sthapak   architect-priest who coordinates the entire mandir construction process

sthapati   chief architect, master builder

sthapatya   architecture

stupi   finial

sutragrahin   chief engineer who implements directions of the *sthapati*

T

takshak sculptor

tala unit of measure

talamana system of proportional measurement

tirth place of pilgrimage

tribhanga triple bend with body gracefully flexed at the neck, shoulders and waist

triratha wall with three projections and recessions from its surface

trishul trident

U

upapitha pedestal; 5 x 5 *vastupurush mandala* grid

upchar item used for worship

urushrung turret attached to the main *shikhar*

utsav festival

utthara beam

V

vahan animal mount or vehicle for a deity

vallabhi type of *nagara shikhar*

varada mudra hand gesture of deity bestowing blessing

varandika entablature

vardhaki stonemason

varna caste

vastu dwelling

vastupurush mandala divine chart used as a basis for generating building designs

vastushastra texts on the science of architecture

vedanga a part of the Vedas

vedibandha base

veena musical instrument

vesara hybrid mandir style incorporating elements of both *nagara* and *dravida* styles

vimana sanctum

vyakhyana mudra hand gesture symbolizing sharing of knowledge

vyala mythical animal

Y

yagna fire sacrifice

yantra auspicious protective diagram

yavai unit of measure equal to the length of a barley rice grain

yoga-nala a hollow copper tube placed in the foundations during the *shilanyas* ceremony that reaches up to the *garbhagruha*

INDEX

Western India 40
mandovar 71
marmas 66
Meenakshi Mandir, Madurai
    38, 39
mithun sculptures 121
moksha 3
mukham 116
Mukteshwar Mandir,
    Bhuvaneshwar 42
mula-prasada. *See* garbhagruha
murti-pratishtha 129
murtis
  alankar 114
  aniconic 107
  ayudha 113
  early 2
  flexions 114
  iconic 106
  jangam 108
  kshanik 108
  making of 109
  materials used for 108
  mudra 112
  posture 112
  sthavar 108
  why? 105–106, 212
  worship of 143–145

N
nagara 21
Nageshvara Mandir, Mosale 29
nature 1
natya mandap 45
natyashastras 111
nirandhara 19

P
pabhaga 44
padhro 25
patotsav 131
patronage 47
Pattadakal 37
pillars
  lathe-turned 40

pitha 69
pradakshina 19, 141
prakara 28, 100
Pramukh Swami Maharaj
  Blessings vi
pranala 78
prasad 213
prasada. *See* garbhagruha
processions 147

R
Rajarani Mandir,
  Bhuvaneshwar 90
ratha 25
Ratha mandirs, Mahabalipuram
  36
roop choki 19

S
sacred space 7
sala 27
samabhanga 114
sandhara 19
shikhar 19, 89
  bhumija 91
  latina 89
  shekhari 90
shilanyas 125–129
shilpashastras 109
site
  initial preparation 63
  purification 63
  selection 59
  testing 60
socle 69
sopana 99
soul 1
sthapak 50
sthapati 50
stupi 28
Surya Mandir, Konark 44
sutragrahin 51

T
takshak 51

tala 116
Teilhard de Chardin, Pierre 1
Teli-ka Mandir, Gwalior 92
Thanjavur 37
tirthyatra 149
toran 87
tribhanga 114

V
varandika 19
vardhaki 51
Vastupurush 65
vastupurush mandala 65–67
vastushastras 55–57
vedibandha 19, 44, 69
vesara 28, 35
Vijayanagara. *See* Hampi
vimana 19, 75
Vitthala Mandir, Vijayanagara
  78
Voltaire 1

W
water tank 100
worship
  personal 3
  tradition 2

Y
yagna altars 31

Shri Akshar Purushottam Maharaj   *Pramukh Swami Maharaj*

BOCHASANWASI SHRI AKSHAR PURUSHOTTAM
SWAMINARAYAN SANSTHA (BAPS)

BAPS is a global socio-spiritual organization committed to the moral and spiritual uplift of mankind. It was established in 1907 CE by Brahmaswarup Shastriji Maharaj in consonance with the Vedic teachings propagated by Bhagwan Swaminarayan (1781-1830 CE). The Sanstha's global network of 1,100 mandirs, 3,850 Satsang centres and 17,000 weekly satsang assemblies (for children, youth and elder devotees) are perennial sources of moral, social, cultural and spiritual activities. The energies of the BAPS volunteer corps of 55,000 youths and over 900 sadhus are channelled towards a variety of philanthropic activities.

BAPS is an NGO in consultative Status with the Economic and Social Council of the United Nations. Its world renowned cultural and spiritual complexes, like Swaminarayan Akshardham in New Delhi and Gandhinagar, and Swaminarayan Mandirs in London, Houston, Chicago, Atlanta, Toronto, Los Angeles, Robbinsville and Nairobi are some of its epoch-making contributions to society.

HIS HOLINESS PRAMUKH SWAMI MAHARAJ

Acclaimed as a unique and rare holy soul of India, His Holiness Pramukh Swami Maharaj was born on 7 December 1921, in the village of Chansad, Gujarat. He is the fifth successor in the illustrious spiritual tradition of Bhagwan Swaminarayan, and the present spiritual head of BAPS and embodiment of the universal Hindu ideals.

Out of his compassion for humanity, he has made over 17,000 village, town and city visits and sanctified over 250,000 homes in India and abroad. He has read and replied to over 700,000 letters, and personally counselled over 810,000 people. He has inspired a cultural, moral and spiritual renaissance in India and abroad by establishing over 1,000 mandirs and grand cultural complexes like Swaminarayan Akshardham in New Delhi and Gandhinagar. Above all, his profound experience and realization of God is the essence of his success and divine lustre.